Stephanie E. Przybylek

with Marie Eckhardt and Jim Richerson

Breaking the Silence On Film

The History of the Case Research Lab

The Cayuga Museum of History and Art
Auburn, New York

The Cayuga Museum
203 Genesee Street
Auburn, New York   13021

Library of Congress Catalogue Card Number: 99-74585

ISBN 0-9673366-1-9

Acknowledgements

Additional thanks to Hal Wallace, Museum Specialist-Electricity Collections, Smithsonian Institution; Betty Lewis, Curator, Seward House; Nichol Forsht, Collections Management Consultant; the staff in the Department of Manuscripts, Cornell University; Randall Crawford and Ted Bartlett, Crawford and Stearns Architects and Preservation Planners; Tom Hunter, Onondaga Historical Association; Marc Wanamaker, Bison Archives; Tom Yaglowski. I also express thanks to Catherine "Mimo" Sponable and members of the Case family, especially Theodore "Bill" Case Jr., for generously sharing family photographs and materials.

My family and friends have been very supportive during this project. I would especially like to thank Nancy Price, Bruce Peacock, George Nickerson and Peter Sanborn for helping me preserve a degree of sanity while this book was being researched and written.

And finally, my thanks to former Cayuga Museum Director Peter Jones, who hired me in the spring of 1994 as curator of the Cayuga Museum when the Case Research Lab was not yet open as a historic site. In his six years as Director of the Cayuga Museum, Peter determinedly pursued the restoration of the Case Research Lab and carriage house sound studio, saving the buildings and the collections in the process. He possessed the tenacity to finally jump-start the process of retrieving this forgotten history, and his work was the foundation on which this project developed.

Introduction

In 1958, Cayuga Museum Director Walter Long wrote to inventor Lee de Forest, exploring the possibility of de Forest's participation in an exhibit on the history of the Case Research Lab. De Forest, from his California home, sent a pleasant response that also managed to convey his opinion of his own role in film history. "Your letter carries me back to the early 'Twenties when I first met Mr. Case," de Forest wrote. "At that time he [Case] knew nothing regarding recording speech and music upon a photographic film. He had something to contribute in the form of a detector responsive to light fluctuations, but unfortunately had a very low frequency response. . . . Of course I am willing to be included in your story of this great development,"[1] With such a statement, made fourteen years after Case's death, de Forest contributed to the misconceptions surrounding Case's role in the invention of sound film.

The collaborative rivalry between Theodore Case of the Case Research Lab and Lee de Forest of De Forest Phonofilms, which disintegrated into conflict and litigation, is a subject worthy of a Hollywood movie. Case succeeded in creating the first commercially successful system of sound-on-film, known as Fox-Case Movietone, only to see his contribution to motion pictures nearly lost to history, which adds poignancy to the drama. It certainly sounds exciting—a young man of wealth, talent, and creativity opens a research lab in his backyard, sells an invention within ten years, makes a million dollars, and lives the high life in the age of Prohibition. But the nuts and bolts process of invention, its tedium and occasional abstract brilliance, is not the glamorous stuff of Hollywood. The Case

Research Lab at the height of its creative years was a place of scientific experimentation, with dedicated men and women spending long hours creating, testing and re-testing products.

The Case-de Forest relationship, which lies at the heart of this story, is problematic. Case and de Forest certainly worked together, and the nature of their collaboration was complex. Both men possessed confidence in their abilities and both freely solicited and accepted advice from the other. De Forest, the elder of the two men, clearly viewed the relationship as that of a superior-subordinate, and he held the advantage of higher name recognition in the United States during the 1920s. Case, independently wealthy and not hesitant about his own scientific skills, came to view de Forest as an inventor/promoter with marginal business acumen.

Many published sources on film history mention Case briefly if at all. Those that do often record his contribution negatively, reporting that he stole de Forest's invention or bested de Forest out of envy. Documentation existing in the Case Research Lab archives clearly proves the inaccuracy of these scenarios. De Forest may have planted the seed in Case's mind concerning commercial application of sound film, but Case clearly succeeded in creating a complete working system, while de Forest failed to do so without heavy assistance—scientific and financial—from the Case Research Lab.

How was the Case Research Lab's role lost to history? Neither Case nor Earl Sponable, Case's chief assistant, were men prone to trumpeting their achievements. After the sound film patents were sold to Fox in 1926, Case increasingly backed away from active involvement in the company. When he died in 1944 he had no direct role in Fox Films. Sponable, quiet and soft-spoken, remained for many years with Fox-Case, which later became Twentieth Century-Fox Film Corporation, as Technical Director of the Research and Development Division. Although Sponable clearly discussed the Case Research Lab's sound-on-film contribution in a 1947 article in the *Journal of the Society of Motion Picture Engineers*, it was not a publication geared to a general audience. For the most part Sponable seemed satisfied to earn the respect of his colleagues in the technical side of the film industry. Lee de Forest, who outlived Case by seventeen years, was as much of a self-promoter as Sponable was not. De Forest spent his later years actively trying to ensure that his name would not be forgotten. He was given an honorary Academy Award for the invention of sound film in 1960, a year before his death in 1961.

Case, an Auburn, New York native, had been an easily recognizable local celebrity in the 1920s and 1930s. Many city residents remembered being invited to watch "Ted's Talkies" in Case's carriage house studio, or attending film showings in a tent on the Auburn Theological Seminary grounds. A mythology grew up surrounding the Case Research Lab in Auburn, even during Case's lifetime. Rumors of Hollywood connections mingled with an image of Case as a wealthy eccentric, a man of scientific genius who enjoyed floating on Owasco Lake in an inner tube, dressed in a white suit with cigar and martini in hand. In the years following Case's death, the facts regarding the Case Research Lab's role in the invention of sound film became increasingly intertwined with fanciful stories.

The Cayuga Museum also played a role in the eclipse of Case's name by not preserving the lab and interpreting its history. When Case helped found the Cayuga Museum in 1936, he did not require his name to be used for the museum building, but he did insist that his role in the invention of Movietone be properly recorded. But perhaps his story was too immediate to be understood in the 1930s and 1940s, too close in time and proximity to those around him to be regarded as "history." Case's equipment went into storage, and the idea of a permanent exhibit dedicated to Case ebbed and flowed periodically, due to many competing interests on the part of Museum Director Walter Long. Preserving the lab as an intact historic site was never worked into the Cayuga Museum's early mission, and it was eventually disassembled. As the years passed and programming continued, Case's laboratory eventually became the museum's art studio, where generations of local residents took painting classes. By the 1960s, many people who entered the building never realized its original purpose or historic significance. Film scholars may have been vaguely familiar with Case's name, but the Case Research Lab collection, including archival materials essential for research purposes, remained unavailable and in storage into the late 1980s. Scholars were unable to gain access to the material, and an important avenue for bringing the Case Research Lab's role into perspective was lost.

This publication is not meant to be the definitive history of the Case Research Lab, but an introduction to the site and its primary players. Case and his associates worked on many projects, but not all directly influenced sound film developments, the primary focus during the lab's peak years of activity. Due to space limitations, some very interesting work has not been discussed here.

The complete history of this site is a very technical one, beyond the scope of this publication. Earl Sponable played an important role in sound film development after his years at the Case Research Lab and is deserving of further research in his own right. The patent wars and corporate wrangling between de Forest, Fox-Case, William Fox and other film industry interests after 1926 are also subjects worthy of closer examination. Such facets of Case Research Lab history and its specific technical components are ripe for scholarly treatment.

I hope *Breaking the Silence on Film* will spark a reassessment of Case's role in the history of sound-on-film and in the fascinating history of a technology that helped to fundamentally change society's view of itself and the world around it.

Stephanie E. Przybylek
March 1, 1999

Chapter 1

The Case Family
and the Scientific Mind

1

The Case Family and the Scientific Mind

The history of the Case Research Lab is also a family history. Theodore Case built his success upon the accomplishments and interests of the generations that preceded him, individuals in whom wealth and science ran as interconnected strains. The Case family arrived in America in 1635 when John Case sailed to the colonies from England aboard the *Dorset*. Four subsequent generations of Cases settled in Connecticut before Erastus Case (1789-1857) changed the family path. Erastus married May Pettibone in 1811, and two children, Jane and Theodore Pettibone, resulted from the union. Erastus relocated to Auburn, New York in 1843 when his daughter Jane married prominent Auburn physician and investor Sylvester Willard. The Willards and Erastus moved into a large Greek Revival house and estate at 203 Genesee Street.

Erastus Case possessed an indomitable spirit and keen business sense. Armed with skills from earlier successful business ventures in Connecticut, he flourished in Auburn. Erastus proved instrumental in establishing Kingsford's Oswego Starch Factory, and his early investment in the company's stock yielded enormous dividends. Erastus then reinvested the funds in Chicago real estate and western railroad stocks and bonds, amassing a family fortune in the process.

The transition from business to scholarship in the Case family occurred with Theodore Pettibone (T. P.) Case (1818-1891), who followed in his father's footsteps for a time, living in Chicago when Erastus pursued business interests in that city. T. P. later served as director of the Lake Shore Railroad, and augmented the family wealth through frugality and wise investment. But business affairs did not consume him, and T. P. dedicated himself to intellectual, scientific, and humanitarian pursuits. He studied the classics, mastered several languages, read voraciously, and kept abreast of the latest scientific discoveries.

In 1856, T. P. Case married Frances Fitch, daughter of Abijah Fitch, one of Auburn's early settlers. Abijah Fitch was a close friend of William Seward, President Abraham Lincoln's Secretary of State, and accompanied him on his trip around the world. T. P. and Frances Fitch Case's two sons, Willard Erastus and Howard, were born into this atmosphere of wealth, intellectual stimulation and adventure.

Willard Erastus Case (1857-1918) took an interest in science a step further than his father. Willard received a law degree from Hamilton College in 1880 and was admitted to the bar, but he never developed a

Willard estate, 203 Genesee Street, mid-19th century. Sylvester Willard, who married Erastus Case's daughter Jane, was among the wealthiest men in Auburn. A greenhouse on his grand estate became the Case Research Lab.

legal practice. Instead, Willard cultivated a fascination for the budding field of electricity, which was quickly changing the course of daily life. Willard immersed himself in scientific experimentation and thought. He developed several theories regarding electricity, which he presented to prominent scientific organizations. In 1886, when only 29, Willard spoke before the Royal Society of London, and demonstrated the conversion of heat energy into mechanical energy using a

Willard E. Case, late nineteenth century.

battery of his own invention. In 1887, Willard presented a paper before the American Institute for Electrical Engineers, and two years later followed with a paper titled "Electrical Energy from Carbon without Heat." In 1893, he received patents for improvements in making aluminum fluosulphate and aluminum compounds.

In 1897, Willard gave a presentation to the British Association for the Advancement of Science, and demonstrated his theories before the New York Electrical Society in New York City. The *New York Sun* covered his successful presentation. Willard demonstrated how oxidation and reduction of hemoglobin, the carrier of oxygen in the blood, produced electricity. Using a wire to connect a test tube of blood to a motor, he rang a bell by the transmitted energy. Willard's electrical theories stirred scientists, but he admitted that they had little practical application. But scientific experimentation rather than practicality was Willard's concern, and that same year, he lectured on luminescence and X-rays before the Cayuga County Medical Society.

Willard married Eva Caldwell in 1878, and the couple had two children, Theodore W. and Dorothy. When T. P. Case died in 1891, Willard Case became responsible for managing the Case family fortune. In 1901, Willard helped consolidate several gas and electric companies into American Light and Traction Company. In 1904, in honor of his parents, Willard presented a new library building to the Seymour Library Association in Auburn.

Willard enjoyed an opulent life-style, befitting his financial status. He divided his time between Auburn, New York City, and Casowasco, his rambling summer estate on Owasco Lake. During the summer months, Willard could often be found on the water, piloting his steamer *Dorothy* or racing his sailboat *El Chico* against members of the Owasco Yacht Club (of which his brother Howard was a member). Ever the engineer, Willard constructed a hydroelectric system at Casowasco, using a stream on the property to provide electricity to the main house. It was the second hydroelectric system in Cayuga County, New York.

Main house at Casowasco, the Case family summer estate on Owasco Lake, late nineteenth century.

At the turn of the twentieth century, polar research and exploration were fashionable, and Willard began developing and testing several theories on the effect of low temperatures on microorganisms. In 1908, Willard wrote to Jacob Schurman, President of Cornell University, proposing to establish a two-year fellowship at Cornell to pursue the topic. Willard included the condition that he would share credit for any publication resulting from the fellow's research. President Schurman told Willard that such a condition would make it impossible for the university to hire someone for the position. As an alternative, Schurman offered university facilities to anyone Willard selected to carry out the project independently.[1]

Frederick Allen, a colleague of Willard's who also reviewed his fellowship proposal, gave Willard similar but coarser advice. Allen told Willard he would receive little protection from patent law, and any hopes for professional recognition for advancements in the field would come to grief. "My advice to you," Allen concluded, "is to build your own biological laboratory, conduct it yourself . . . publish your own memoirs of this work, or present them to the learned societies by your own hand, out of your own laboratory as you . . . do in your other researches."[2] In his letter, Allen also mentioned conversations with Blin Sill Cushman, Willard's assistant. Cushman, an 1893 Cornell graduate with a B.A. in chemistry, worked in Cornell's Chemistry Department, and later for the Institute of Chemistry at Cornell until 1907. Willard and Cushman became acquainted through Willard's

Theodore Pettibone Case poses with grandson Theodore W. Case, 1889.

scientific work. When Willard traveled, he and Cushman corresponded on a variety of subjects, including genetics (Willard was briefly interested in crossbreeding chickens to develop a more disease-resistant strain).

Theodore Case, three years old, 1892.

Willard's son Theodore, born in 1888, grew up amid his family's wealth and his father's scientific interests. As was customary for the family's social status, Theodore attended East Coast boarding schools, including The Manlius School near Syracuse, New York, and Cloyne House School in Newport, Rhode Island. He finished his secondary education at St. Paul School in Concord, New Hampshire, where he belonged to the Old Hundred intramural football team and the Scientific Club. He didn't excel in athletics, but Theodore's classmates voted him president of the Scientific Club his senior year in 1908. Upon graduation, Theodore headed to Yale University.

Theodore enjoyed the trappings of wealth, and as a young man displayed a penchant for anything that moved fast. "I don't want that car in any races," Willard warned his son in 1910, referring to a Renault convertible Theodore drove at Yale.[3] Also that year, Willard chastised his son for damaging the propellers of a family motorboat while racing it down the Owasco Outlet during low water levels.

Theodore also clearly inherited his father's love of science. While at Yale in 1910, Theodore recorded in a notebook under the heading "To do Someday" three theories he wanted to test. They involved light and magnetism. In January 1911, Theodore expressed interest in transmitting and reproducing sound. He wrote to his mother that he was experimenting with a selenium cell, trying to photograph sound waves and use the positives as records for a new kind of phonograph, or a "lightograph," as he called it.[4]

Theodore wrote to his mother again in February 1911:

> Yesterday I at last succeeded in transmitting sound by light.
> I used the principle of the manometric flame. The eye could
> not detect the variation of the light at all but it was captured
> perfectly in the varying resistance of the selenium. My repro-
> duction of the voice was perfect. Next, I have to set up an
> apparatus for very delicate photographing of the light variations.
> It is very interesting work.[5]

Theodore graduated with a B.A. from Yale in 1912. Willard Case
wanted his son to go to law school, despite his own strong scientific
interest, because it was the customary educational path for a young man
of Case's social standing. Theodore complied, half-heartedly studying
law at Harvard for about a year. But he found scientific research far
more alluring. In 1914, accepting the inevitable, Willard and his son set
up laboratories in the basement of their homes at 196 Genesee Street
and Casowasco.

In May 1916, Willard Case inherited the grand Willard estate at 203
Genesee Street. The elder Case remained at
196 Genesee Street, and Theodore
moved into the house where his
great-grandfather Erastus had
lived upon his arrival in
Auburn. Willard and
Theodore converted the
remains of a greenhouse at
203 Genesee Street into a
scientific laboratory, and
the Case Research Lab was
born, substantially supported
by the Case family fortune.
Such financial backing
proved crucial to the lab's

Willard-Case mansion, 203 Genesee Street,
late nineteenth century.

Self-portrait, Theodore Case with camera, circa 1908.

success, because Theodore spent roughly $100,000 per year to operate it.[6] Cushman became the Case Research Lab's first employee. Possibly through Cushman's connections, the Cases hired another Cornell graduate, Earl Iru Sponable, to help design the lab and assist Theodore with experiments. Sponable, a promising young scientist, had just received his B.A. in chemistry from Cornell in the spring of 1916.

Theodore Case and Earl Sponable formed the core of the Case Research Lab scientific team. These two men were worlds apart; Theodore, born to wealth and society, and Earl, a farm boy from Plainfield, New York, who had worked his way through Cornell playing violin and waiting tables.[7] Both men however, were brilliant and hard working. Despite their differences, or perhaps because of them, they made a winning combination.

Willard Case proudly followed his son's research. When one or the other traveled, father and son corresponded regularly, and Willard often gave Theodore encouragement and advice. On one letter, Willard scrawled over the first page "Keep this," as he tried to understand how a light sensitive cell that Ted developed worked.[8] In another letter, Willard wrote:

> I assume you know the terms you are using in your paper. . . .
> Suppose you said two theories one photoelectric and the other
> chemical. . . . On this theory you produce electrolysis in the cell
> by light. . . . In an electrolytic cell copper is transferred from
> anode to cathode <u>but</u> not the electro chemical equivalent as

gravity interferes. You have struck a most wonderful discovery.[9]

In the letter's postscript, Willard commented, "This reasoning has made me so nervous I have tried to write as fast as I think."

Willard served as Theodore's mentor and champion, and he took it upon himself to critique other colleagues' interpretations of his son's discoveries. In September 1916, Willard wrote to George Guy of the New York Electrical Society:

Exterior, Case Research Lab, circa 1916, with Willard-Case mansion in the background.

I noted the article in the 'London Electrician' which you sent. I haven't any authority to speak for Ted as he isn't here. The author has evidently jumped before he got to the fence. He is . . . one of the literary fellows who has a smattering of photo-electric effect. Let me try to make it clear to you. . . . Ted's effects were not the same as the others. He has found so many new and interesting things . . . in the way that the current goes, and the strength of the current, which is an important thing, and, by the way, he has got more current than anyone else. . . . This morning he has found a substance which will take the place of selenium which varies its resistance when light strikes it when it is in a dry state. His method, which is being written up for publication, is the using of a wireless detector and magnifier for discerning these reactions, which is a great step in advance for the purpose of investigations for physicists and chemists. Criticism is a good thing because it gives him an idea of just where he stands in relation to others.[10]

Willard and Theodore Case possessed fundamental scientific insight and curiosity, something no advanced degree or formal training could give them. The relatively new field of electricity fascinated both men, and they knew that to advance in the field they needed to be well versed in the subject. By example, advice, and with the decided advantage of family wealth, Willard Case set the stage for his son. In 1916, Theodore Case and the newly christened Case Research Lab were ready to pursue the limelight.

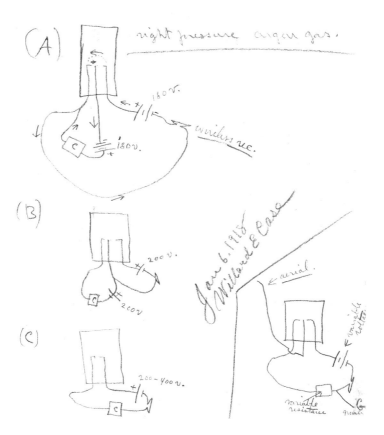

Drawing by Willard Case, 1918.

Chapter 2

Pure Science and Infrared Rays:
Lab Beginnings, 1916-1919

2

Pure Science and Infrared Rays: Lab Beginnings, 1916-1919

At the New York Electrical Society's annual meeting on June 14, 1916, Theodore Case presented a paper titled "Preliminary Notes on a New Way of Converting Light into Electrical Energy." In it, he detailed experiments in photoelectricity, generating energy by letting the sun shine on a large cell:

> I . . . put two copper plates in a solution of diluted salt water. . . .
> To each plate is attached a wire, as in an ordinary electric
> battery, and to measure the current the other ends of the wire
> are fastened to a galvanometer. One plate of ordinary polished
> copper is kept in the dark. The plate in front of it, of black
> oxidized copper, is exposed to the light—preferably to strong
> sunlight. And there is no question that a current is set up.[1]

Case's ideas provoked discussion in scientific publications and the regional press. Several sources noted that although his work was purely scientific, such experimentation could lead to big things. The young inventor created something of a stir, as reflected in comments from *The Evening World*:

> It was Emerson who dreamily advised you to hitch your wagon
> to a star, but tomorrow you may, quite literally and practically,
> hitch your motor car to the sun. Also your vacuum cleaner,
> your coffee percolator, your electric hair tongs. . . .

For there are certainly all these golden and boundless possibilities in the just announced discovery of Theodore W. Case, who seems on the way to being Thomas Edison No. 2. He is only twenty-six years old, and his father, Willard E. Case, is worth $20,000,000. Yet, despite these handicaps, young Mr. Case has found a way of extracting electricity from the sun, which created a sensation among the members of the New York Electrical Society, whom he addressed at their annual meeting the other night.[2]

Case must have been pleased with the response. He saved the article, meeting notice, and press clippings, and added them to a scrapbook he started on June 16, 1916, two days after he gave the paper.

Photoelectricity experiments dominated Case Research Lab activities throughout 1916 and into 1917. Case, Sponable, and Cushman repeatedly tested minerals, many from Willard Case's collection, for photoactivity. To facilitate these experiments, Case bought receiving sets and an audion amplifier from De Forest Radio Telephone & Telegraph Company. When he requested specific data regarding the smallest pulsating current that could be detected and amplified with the device, a company representative responded sheepishly, "We regret to advise you that owing to the congested condition in our laboratory and factory, it is impossible to do any research . . . "[3] Case later wrote to Lee de Forest himself, requesting a visit to talk to the inventor about the question his company couldn't answer.

Theodore Case in the yard of 203 Genesee Street with copper cell device, 1916. Photoelectricity experiments dominated early Case Research Lab activities.

In early 1917, Case purchased additional mineral specimens and used the audion amplifier to detect signals from crystals. He and his assistants carried out repeated tests with a galvanometer and recorded changes minute-by-minute for hours—sometimes even at 2:00 AM, which certainly reflected youthful enthusiasm. Willard Case remained involved in an advisory

Earl Sponable with copper cell device, 1916.

capacity, and Sponable recalled reporting back to him at least once.[4]

Case followed the traditional route to developing a professional reputation by publishing in scientific journals. In April 1917, his "Notes on the Change of Resistance of Certain Substances in Light" appeared in the *Physical Review*, followed by "A Cuprous Oxide Photo-Chemical Cell" in the *American Electrochemical Society*. But when the United States entered World War I on April 6, 1917, Case put aside sunlight experiments and shifted his lab's focus to finding wartime applications of photoelectric principles.

Case and his assistants received favorable results with dyscracite, a mineral containing a combination of antimony, lead, and sulfur, with traces of mercury, silver, and arsenic. When tested, they found dyscracite exhibited more photoactivity in the longer red rays than most crystals, and Case realized it could be used to detect infrared light. Lab assistants constructed crude light detecting cells with bits of dyscracite mounted to a cork base and held in place with gold leaf paste.

Case and his associates improvised their first attempt at signaling in early 1917. They used a 12-inch searchlight powered by two electric trolley cars on South Street Road near Auburn. Bad weather and equipment problems contributed to poor results. Undaunted, they held a second test closer to home, sending signals from the barn of the Case home at 196 Genesee Street, and receiving them at a station on the second floor of the old Willard mansion. This time, they successfully detected signals.

In the spring, Case tried unsuccessfully to send underwater messages on Owasco Lake between the dock at Casowasco and a point a half-mile away, the experiments being hampered by fog and rough waters. Case and Sponable worked on the system throughout the summer, placing additional experimental signaling and receiving units on houses in Auburn and in the nearby towns of Throop and Aurelius. Local residents must have wondered about the young inventors, scurrying about mounting searchlights and other contraptions on building roofs, and involved in continual activity without visible results.

Signaling with infrared rays had been theoretically possible for several years, but until 1916 it had not been practical. Case's proposed system combined three features: a high intensity arc searchlight (rich in infrared radiation) manufactured by Sperry Gyroscope Company, an Eastman Kodak infrared filter that screened out most of the visible spectrum, and a stable quick responding detector cell that picked up infrared rays. Case contacted Sperry Gyroscope Company to propose tests.[5]

Case's sending unit included a searchlight, infrared filter, and hand-operated shutter. The infrared filter, made of a treated gelatin sheet mounted between glass, was attached to the front of the searchlight. By looking directly into the searchlight, one could see only a faint red light. An operator used the shutter, set up in front of the searchlight and filter and resembling a large venetian blind, to flash Morse code signals. The receiving unit consisted of a photoelectric cell mounted at the focus of a parabolic reflector, which concentrated the infrared rays on the cell. The reflector was attached to a portable box with batteries. Initially, lab personnel used a galvanometer to detect the infrared signals. Later they changed this part of the system to use a more practical telephone or wireless receiver.

Case, Sponable, Cushman, and Sperry Co. personnel successfully tested the system in New York City from stations on the Sperry building roof and Woolworth Building in Manhattan, and Prospect Park Reservoir in Brooklyn. In May 1917, Case was summoned to Washington D. C. by General George O. Squier of the U. S. Army Signal Corps, who expressed interest in possible military applications. On October 18, 1917, Case Research Lab and military personnel staged the first formal demonstration of the system, across an eighteen-mile stretch of New York Harbor between Fort Hancock at Sandy Hook, New Jersey, and the 50th floor of the Woolworth Building. Witnesses to the test included Elmer Sperry Sr. of Sperry Gyroscope Co, and the Naval Consulting Board, comprised of Navy and Army officers.

While becoming increasingly involved in military work, Case and his assistants continued experimenting with substances in the lab. In October

Interior of Case Research Lab, 1916-1918. This view shows the appearance of the lab during work with the infrared system, prior to building additions in 1918. The wall with a curtain and shelves of chemical bottles were removed to facilitate more laboratory space.

1917, Case began working with thallium salts and then thallium sulfide, which he found sensitive to infrared light. Case immediately proceeded to patent his find. The photoelectric cell that resulted from these experiments became known as the Thalofide Cell for its composition of thallium, oxygen, and sulfur, the material prepared by slightly oxidizing it, fusing it onto a heated ³/4 inch quartz disc, and placing it in an evacuated tube. Initially used in the infrared signaling system, the Thalofide Cell would prove increasingly important in later projects.

On February 7, 1918, Case Lab personnel formally tested the signaling system for the Coast Defense Board at Fort Monroe, Virginia. They mounted a sending device on a searchlight tower and a receiving unit on the tug *Reno*. While at Fort Monroe, Case brainstormed possible uses for his system, including for communication between ships in a transport convoy, to help ships in distress, and for general harbor defense. He proposed it as a solution to the lighthouse problem along the British coast,

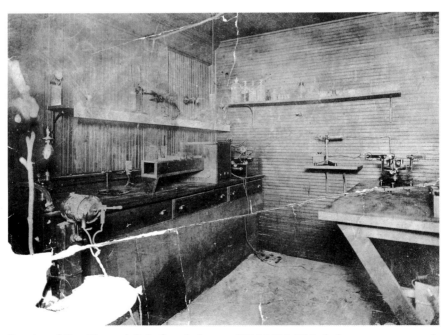

Interior of Case Research Lab, first darkroom, 1916-1918. This darkroom was removed by the middle of 1918. Some of the equipment still exists in the museum collection.

where lighthouses darkened to avoid detection by enemy parties made safe coastline navigation by home ships difficult. Case believed his system could act as a way to help negotiate minefields, as a portable unit for trench work, and as a nighttime communication system for submarines recharging on the surface.

Successful Fort Monroe demonstrations caught the attention of Major R. A. Millikan of the National Research Council, who sent Case to the Naval Experimental Station at New London, Connecticut. The Navy's Engineering Department also expressed interest in Case, and they offered him a commission in the Engineering Corps, which he declined. For the rest of the war, Case and Sponable served as civilian associates at New London, frequently traveling back and forth by train between Auburn and Connecticut. They held many subsequent shipboard tests to improve equipment watertightness in fog and rain, and worked to design a system stable enough to operate even in rough seas. Meanwhile, military personnel demonstrated the signaling system in France, England, and Italy.

In April 1918, Case, Sponable, and several military representatives left port at New Haven to witness signaling tests with a squadron of submarine chasers. They ran into the stormy weather of a northeast gale, resulting in badly maneuvered tests and seasickness for nearly everyone except Case. "Due either to careful preliminary preparation or vigorous physical make-up," Case recalled jauntily, he "suffered none of the ill effects so common to most members of the crew."[6] When the boats pulled up anchor and returned home the following morning, all parties

Infrared signaling system, sending unit with blind, circa 1917.

must have been very relieved. In May, Case and Charles H. Steel, another lab assistant, participated in demonstrations at New London that were witnessed by, among others, Thomas Edison.[7]

Case began seeking patents for these devices in early 1918. In response to his requests, the Federal Trade Commission informed Case that issuing the patents would be withheld during the war, and:

> You are hereby notified that your application as above identified has been found to contain subject matter which might be detrimental to the public safety or assist the enemy in this present war, and you are hereby ordered to in no wise publish the invention or disclose the subject matter of said application, except that the invention may be disclosed to Officials of the War and Navy Departments of the United States. . . . [8]

Another letter outlined a $10,000 fine and maximum imprisonment of ten years in violation of the order. All of Case's patent applications received the same response.

Taking the warning seriously, Case required his office and shop employees, mostly young women, to sign a form binding them to complete secrecy regarding inventions being developed at the lab. "The undersigned solemnly swears not to speak to anyone at all of what she had learned or heard at the Laboratory, not even to her family, ... " each employee read before dutifully committing their signature to paper.

While wartime work continued, the lab expanded in both physical space and manpower to meet increasing production needs. In 1918 Case added a new darkroom, office spaces, and a chemical storage room. Walls in the main laboratory were torn out to accommodate more equipment. Case's assistants built and installed an eight-foot photometer in the darkroom for testing cells.

Case, Cushman, Sponable, and Steel, who was an Auburn native and Williams College graduate, formed the core of the lab research team, and by 1918 the lab employed at least ten additional men and women as mechanics, machinists, glass blowers, and secretaries. Alice Gertrude

Eldred, the daughter of a respected Auburn merchant, worked as a glassblower and lab assistant for $5 a week upon her graduation from Auburn High School in 1917. She evidently caught Case's eye, and Gertrude, as she was more often called, became his wife in 1918. Margaret Tryon, and Rosamond and Beatrice Eldred, Gertrude's sisters, listed themselves as laboratorians in city directories. Frank Steigerwald served as Case's electrician, and three other men, mentioned only as Gill, Owens, and Hall, did carpentry and other work. These men and women continued testing batches of light cells, practiced their

Alice Gertrude Eldred, later Gertrude Case, in front of the Case Research Lab, circa 1918.

skill at glass blowing, and carried out the tedious precision work that was the core of lab production—tracking data, grinding bases for light cells, gilding surfaces of bases, and assembling cells.

Even Willard Case remained active in his son's scientific endeavors, conducting tests for parraffining wood needed to produce signaling system boxes. Sadly, Willard died in late 1918, a victim of the Spanish Influenza epidemic that swept through the United States. Theodore did not write about his father's passing, or record it in his scrapbook, but he preserved many pieces of Willard's early electrical equipment as cherished keepsakes.

Eventually, Case began to experiment by sending infrared messages via voice by manometric flame rather than by Morse code dots and dashes. In April 1918, Case set up a voice transmission apparatus using a manometric flame placed at the focus of an 11-inch reflector, the flame burning at the height of one-half inch. Whispers were readily heard using this system. That same month, Sponable visited General Electric

Company, in Schenectady, New York, to discuss the problem of changing voice variations into electrical modulations, and he filed their suggestions with ideas to be returned to following the war.[9] Case, meanwhile, talked to Western Electric representatives regarding loudspeaker apparatus for the signaling system.

In October, Sponable and Cushman participated in nighttime tests on the U.S.S. Arizona and U.S.S. Pennsylvania off the Atlantic coast near New London. After the World War I armistice came on November 11, 1918, Case continued to pursue military uses for lab inventions, promoting the creation of a four-mile portable signal system for the Army. The Navy conducted further signaling tests with Case's system while the fleet was en route to Guantanamo Bay, Cuba, in early 1919.

Unidentified Case Research Lab assistant with large infrared filter, circa 1918. The panes of glass were coated with red gelatin. This filter still exists in the museum collection.

But with the war over, military interests eventually shifted to other needs. The Naval Experimental Station closed in 1919, and Sponable traveled to New London one final time to salvage any remaining equipment. Some pieces of Case's infrared system became part of the Smithsonian Institution's collection in June 1919, when a military consultant gathering material on wartime signaling included a Case Research Lab receiving mirror and dyscracite tubes in a donation to the War Collection. Sponable acknowledged the gift and sent a few more cells.[10]

Accelerated in development due to war, the infrared system proved a timely and crucial success for the young inventors. It set the stage for future Case Research Lab work, allowing Case and Sponable to gain experience in the practical application of scientific theories. Several of the companies and individuals with whom they had worked in the creation of this invention would become important players in later projects. These included Eastman Kodak, Bausch & Lomb, Western Electric, General Electric, and perhaps most importantly Lee de Forest of De Forest Radio Telephone & Telegraph Company.

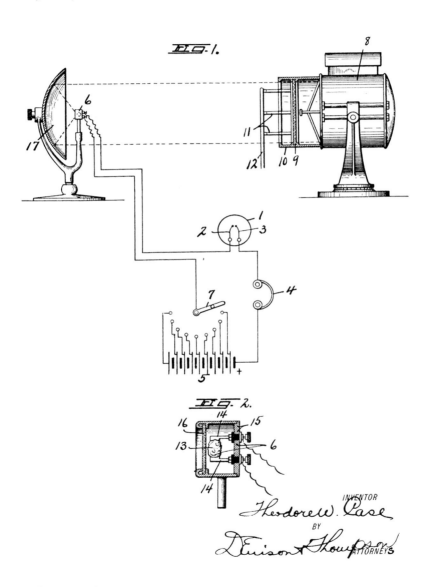

T. W. CASE.
SIGNALING SYSTEM.
APPLICATION FILED FEB. 20, 1916.

1,369,781.

Patented Mar. 1, 1921.

Patent drawing, infrared signaling system, 1916.

Chapter 3

A Search
for Direction

3

A Search
for Direction

In the years following World War I, the Case Research Lab pursued a variety of projects simultaneously, and in the early 1920s Case and his associates seemed to search for direction. They proposed various ideas and carried out assorted experiments, including conducting tests to search for materials active to gamma rays and X-rays, and using lab apparatus to listen for messages from Mars. They received no messages from distant worlds, although "the twinkling of the stars was plainly evident."[1] Lab scientists tried to determine the drift of the earth through the use of ether, tested minerals with radium to see which demonstrated phosphorescence, and conducted experiments with quartz rods and radium to kill streptococci germs.[2] Case even theorized about a connection between the human eye's sensitivity to green and man's evolving from fishes.[3] True to Case's inquisitive nature, any idea with a hint of scientific validity was pursued, at least to a point of generating an initial response.

While these sometimes-whimsical experiments punctuated the lab's creative activity, three ideas were pursued for possible commercial/practical applications: the infrared signaling system, the Thalofide Cell, and a daylight recording system. Case, Sponable, Steel, and Cushman traveled throughout the eastern seaboard, juggling their roles as scientists with probably less comfortable roles as salespeople for their products.

Case continued to believe that the military could benefit from his infrared system. In January 1920, Cushman and Sponable went to

Infrared system, prototype of portable system designed for U.S. Army, circa 1919.

Washington D.C. to demonstrate the infrared system to the Signal Corps. In typical bureaucratic military fashion, a successful demonstration resulted in passing the apparatus for more tests to the Equipment Department. In March, a Balloon Air Service lieutenant visited Auburn to explore using the system for signaling to and from balloons. He arranged a test at the Army Balloon fields in Omaha, Nebraska.[4] Cushman returned to Washington for further talks with the military. The Balloon Division eventually decided the system wasn't practical for its purposes.[5]

In early 1920, the lab published a pamphlet advertising the Thalofide Cell. It outlined the cell's sensitivity, spectral analysis, possible uses, and prices, as well as a notice that it would be sold only for experimental purposes. The lab also advertised the product in *Science* magazine, and published a brief article in *Popular Science*, "Insulator in the Dark—Conductor in the Light," which highlighted recent Case Research Lab inventions.

These years also brought changes in Sponable and Case's personal lives. One of Sponable's responsibilities at the Case Research Lab was to record lab experiments and test results. Afraid that he could not keep up with taking notes, Sponable enrolled in a shorthand and typing class at a local night school. Another member of the class, a young woman named Marie Whalen, wanted to improve her standing from a $7 a week clerk in a local grocery store. Sponable and Marie shared a common interest in music: she played piano, and he still owned the violin that had helped him finance his college education. They began meeting in their free to time to play music, and were married in Auburn in late 1918, the same year as the Cases.[6] Theodore and Gertrude Case's first child, Theodore Jr., was born in 1920, followed by a daughter, Barbara, in 1921, and two more children, Jane and John, in the later 1920s.[7]

In August 1920, Lee de Forest wrote to the Case Research Lab, requesting information on the Thalofide Cell. A lab assistant sent him the advertising pamphlet in response.

Earl Sponable, circa 1920.

De Forest wrote again, inquiring if Case had compared his Thalofide Cell and the Kuntz photoelectric cell, which de Forest had been using in sound recording experiments. De Forest also ordered a Thalofide Cell, but one of Case's assistants wrote him that he would not receive it until the lab reopened on September 7th, following its annual vacation shutdown. Impatient, de Forest wrote twice more, and for the first time directed a letter to "Dr. Case," in which he broached the subject of the lab doing experimental work for him:

Photograph courtesy Theodore "Bill" Case Jr.

Theodore Case with Theodore (Bill) Junior, 1920. Case and his wife eventually had four children—Bill, Barbara, Jane, and John.

Breaking the Silence

> Possibly, if you have to make up a new cell to fill our order,
> you can, knowing the proposed method of use and shape of the
> beam of light we are using, design the glass envelope especially
> for our purpose.[8]

De Forest persisted with questions and letters before Case finally answered him. "For the present small order, it would be impractical for us to make up a special cell. However, if in the future, you find that you can use a considerable number of these cells, we might be able to make them specially for you."[9] De Forest proved less persistent in paying his bills, and the lab sent several invoices before receiving compensation. When he finally mailed a check, de Forest claimed the delay due to oversight.[10] Fortunately, Case had other clients, and requests for Thalofide Cells came from as far away as Spezia, Italy.[11]

The Case Research Lab's third commercial venture may have begun through a research request. In early 1920, Kleerflax Linen Rug Company inquired whether the lab had measured daylight falling on material such as fabric. The request sent Case back to investigating daylight, which had first interested him in the copper cell experiments before World War I. The system that resulted used a Case Research Lab strontium or barium photoelectric cell, attached to a Leeds & Northrup potentiometer.

Theodore Case and Earl Sponable in the Case Research Lab, circa 1920.

Daylight recording experiment on grounds of 203 Genesee Street, 1920-1921.

Early in 1920, Sponable went to Philadelphia to discuss cooperative work with Leeds & Northrup in marketing the daylight recording system. By 1921, practical applications were being discussed for the device. Case proposed a long list of potential uses, depending on whether the device worked in both natural and artificial light. Possible venues for the system included weather bureaus, agricultural experimentation stations, automobile headlight testing facilities, street lighting projects (where it could be used to keep records of light levels to determine if companies were fulfilling their contracts), and the dye industry, where the device could help measure fading in fabrics.

While work on the system progressed, Sponable returned to Philadelphia for further talks with Leeds & Northrup representatives, who suggested that Case begin advertising the apparatus by publishing an article about it.[12] They also recommended that the lab measure and record daylight daily for one month from dusk to dawn. Monitors in this time-consuming task included Earl Sponable, and Theodore and Gertrude Case. Following Leeds & Northrup's advice, Case published "New Strontium &

Barium Photo-Electric Cells" in the *American Physical Society Journal* in 1921, and quickly followed with Case Research Lab Bulletin No. 3, which featured the daylight recording system and elaborated on possible uses.

Despite requests from Leeds & Northrup to keep the price of the device down, the Case Research Lab sold the strontium cells with a socket for $200 each, the automatic recorder for an additional $250, and resistance elements and batteries for $40. On the local media front, Case gained coverage in Auburn and nearby Syracuse papers by using the daylight recording system to test the efficiency of different types of streetlights being proposed for use in Auburn.[13]

The daylight recording system generated initial excitement, but quickly ran into problems. Leeds & Northrup found that increasingly, the photoelectric cells were not remaining constant. Sponable returned to Philadelphia to meet with company officials about possible solutions to the

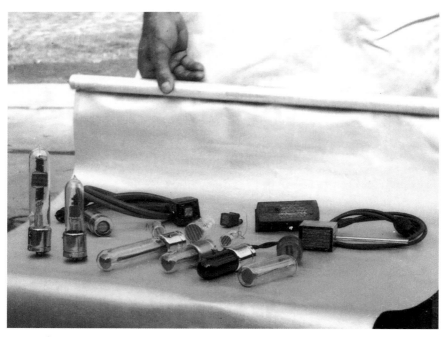

Array of light cells made by Case Research Lab, 1920s. The rectangular cells near the back right of this impromptu display were early dyscracite experiments. Several of these cells still exist in the museum collection.

problem, and he, Case, and Cushman conducted repeated tests, varying chemical compositions and preparation of the cells to try and correct the instability. As 1921 ended, they began testing the large cells with various colored filters. The lab also continued to manufacture Thalofide Cells, but reluctantly abandoned the signaling system, realizing that demand for it was limited outside of military purposes.[14]

HIGH VACUUM STRONTIUM PHOTO-ELECTRIC CELL

BULLETIN No. 3
1921

CASE RESEARCH LABORATORY

AUBURN, N. Y.

High Vacuum Strontium Photo-Electric Cell, Bulletin No. 3, 1921. These large cells were sold for use in the daylight recording system.

May 15, 1923.   1,455,074

T. W. CASE

APPARATUS FOR RECORDING LIGHT

Filed Dec. 11, 1920   4 Sheets—Sheet 2

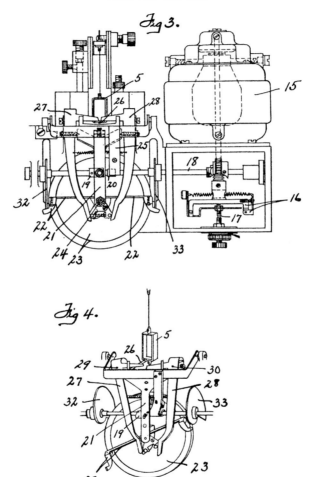

Patent drawing; apparatus for recording light, filed Dec. 11, 1920.

Chapter 4

Enter
Lee de Forest

4

Enter
Lee de Forest

By early 1922, progress on commercializing Case Research Lab inventions had stalled. With the daylight system proving unsatisfactory and the signaling system set aside, lab personnel concentrated on manufacturing Thalofide Cells, testing the large barium cells with colored filters, and compiling lists of cell numbers, light conditions, and calculations. Case, Cushman, Steel, and Sponable continued pursuing various experimental ideas and possibilities, but without a central focus. They were ready for a new direction, and an earlier acquaintance, Lee de Forest, provided it.

De Forest had been using Thalofide Cells in sound film work since his initial request to the lab in 1920. While Case had begun making a name for himself in the early 1920s, de Forest already enjoyed widespread recognition as a scientist and inventor, predominantly for his audion tube and pioneering work in radio. Cultivated and accomplished, de Forest was also a showman known for a fierce pride and condescending view of those around him.[1] De Forest had begun working on sound film in 1918 (he had been experimenting with sound tests since 1913), and he filed patents for inventions related to that process by 1919. In 1921, he and his family traveled to Germany, where he pursued the invention of Phonofilm, his sound-on-film system, and attempted to invent a high frequency discharge tube.[2]

Case followed de Forest's progress and was aware of his claims surrounding talking motion pictures. Case clipped and pasted into his scrapbook a brief newspaper article from April 1922, which heralded

Lee de Forest in German film studio, circa 1919. This image appeared in *Radio News* in November 1925.

"Talking Movies Perfected, Wireless Pioneer Claims." The article discussed de Forest's experiments, and his return to New York City from Germany. "He has used my Thal. Cells," Case scribbled in red pencil along the edge of the article.[3]

De Forest's quest for a workable sound-on-film system involved several key components. To record sound films, de Forest needed a microphone to accurately pick up sound and a camera with a sensitive modulating light source to act as the recording mechanism. The light source translated sound into pulses of electricity that could be recorded on a piece of film. The sound track appeared as fine lines of alternating dark and light bands. To reproduce the films, de Forest needed a projector with a sound attachment—the film ran in front of a small light bulb, which illuminated the sound track. A photoelectric cell then translated the sound track back into pulses of electricity, which would then be greatly amplified, producing the sound that had originally been recorded.

Inventors had been experimenting with sound recording since 1857. Eugen Augustin Lauste, a former Edison employee, created a primitive sound-on-film system by 1904, and demonstrated a synchronized system in England in 1913. That same year, Elias E. Ries applied for patents relating to recording sound film, which were granted in 1923. Joseph Tykociner, a professor at the University of Illinois, successfully demonstrated a system that the New York press covered in June 1922.[4] But none of the systems proved commercially feasible.

And the motion picture industry regarded sound films with scorn. Although movies had mushroomed into one of the fifteen largest industries in the United States by the 1920s, the major Hollywood studios, through fears of capital costs and doubts about sound film ever being more than a novelty, were reticent to pursue talkies. Silent films reached their creative peak in the 1920s—features between 1922 and 1926 included *Orphans of the Storm*, *Greed*, *The Gold Rush*, and *The Phantom of the Opera*, with stars such as Charlie Chaplin and Lon Chaney, Sr. In promoting a technology that the major studios dismissed, and one that would fundamentally change the nature of film, de Forest faced an uphill battle. But he firmly believed that sound film was the future, and was determined to reach the public with Phonofilm. Case's Thalofide Cell had proved invaluable in the final part of the process, accurately reproducing de Forest's early crude sound films.[5]

While de Forest pursued a solution to the sound film puzzle, Case continued to write and

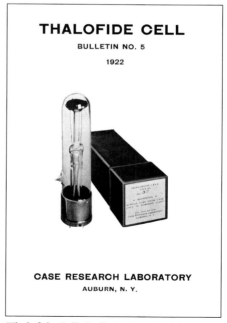

Thalofide Cell, Bulletin No. 5, 1922. A copy of the bulletin Lee de Forest received when he first inquired about the Thalofide Cell.

Exterior, Case Research Lab, early 1920s.

publish in scientific journals. "Infra Red Telegraphy & Telephony" appeared in the *Journal of Optical Society of America* in June, followed in August by an article on photoelectric material and thermoelectric currents in audion bulbs. Still, Case followed de Forest's progress. In September 1922, he pasted a *New York Times* article into his scrapbook that highlighted de Forest's explanation of his new talking films. Along the edge, Case again scribbled, "He is using my thalofide cells." Did the young inventor keep these articles to highlight his own contribution, or was he already uncertain of credit due in any de Forest collaboration? If the latter, his concern would prove well founded.

In September 1922, Case informed de Forest that the Case Research Lab had developed a new cell that combined the sensitivity of the Thalofide Cell with improvements that created a very quiet cell for sound reproduction.[6] Case invited de Forest to try the new product. Knowing the quality of the Thalofide Cells, de Forest responded favorably and invited Case to New York. The men met and discussed Case's new invention at the Ambassador Hotel on October 2.[7]

Case sailed for London the following day. While abroad, he witnessed a demonstration of another sound film system, which he later claimed spurred his interest to pursue sound film.[8] Upon returning to the United States, Case again stopped at de Forest's studio, where he viewed and heard examples of de Forest's talking pictures. They discussed improvements to the Thalofide Cells, and de Forest's use of Case Research Lab products in his sound film system. The two inventors made arrangements to alter production of cells to eliminate a frying noise heard during sound transmission. They thought it came from graphite lines on the quartz disc inside the light cell.

The relationship of Case and de Forest began as one of colleagues mutually involved in the give and take of scientific exchange. They created no formal agreements specifying the nature of their collaboration. As contact between the two increased, a clear pattern in their working relationship emerged: de Forest would propose a problem, sometimes sending suggestions, technical notes and drawings to Case. He would then ask Case and his team to solve it. Another of de Forest's traits, impatience, displayed itself clearly during this period. De Forest pressed for things to be done quickly. "We are 'shooting' almost every day," he wrote to Case, "so I will greatly appreciate quick action!"[9] De Forest's correspondence constantly urged speed as he pushed to get his sound film system into production, a pattern counter to the methodical approach of Case and his team. The informal nature of de Forest and Case's working relationship would later come back to haunt both parties, when legal ramifications and competing claims of invention demanded clearer boundaries than those they had originally set.

By November, the Case Research Lab was fully engaged in making and testing cells for sound film reproduction. Lab scientists sent cells back and forth between de Forest's studio and the Case Research Lab, and corresponded regularly regarding changes, drawings of ideas, improvements, and problems with experimental equipment. On November 20, de Forest telegrammed Case, "NEW CELL GIVES NO SCRATCH WHATEVER IS GREAT IMPROVEMENT OVER ALL OTHERS BY ALL MEANS." It signaled a definite step forward, although they still heard background noise when the film was played. Case tested the cells again and invited de Forest to Auburn to witness the tests. De Forest suggested to Case that the noise might be from graininess in the emulsion of developed film, a question he also proposed to Eastman Kodak representatives.

So Case began experimenting on the film to determine the source of background noise. Lab associates tested Thalofide Cells to see how much noise was coming from the cells and how much from the film base itself. Under a microscope, they found specks of dust or debris that had adhered to the film surface during manufacture. To see how varying film thickness affected the recording process, Case and his staff ran the film through a makeshift camera, using the manometric flame as the recording mechanism.[10] They found the thicker the film base, the quieter the results. "This immediately raises the question," Case wrote to de Forest, "as to whether Eastman could make you some film base say half as thick again as what you have. We might find this to be very much quieter."[11]

The lab also continued searching for a possible light source to act as the catalyst in recording voice transmissions. De Forest told Case he had been using very small flashlight bulbs for taking pictures of sound. The small bulbs proved unsatisfactory, because de Forest had to burn them very brightly, which wore them out quickly. Case had earlier suggested using hydrogen in the bulbs, and in December de Forest asked him to try the idea. Case sent the finished examples to de Forest's New York City studio, along with some small surgical bulbs from Welch-Allyn, a surgical tool manufacturing company in Auburn. None proved satisfactory.

On December 14, following the unsuccessful flashlight bulb trials, Case shifted to the idea of a gas glow discharge, an idea that de Forest had earlier abandoned. Case considered creating a tube in which the gas would be in a ready state, with electrodes closer together, resulting in impulses that would be more easily ionized and discharged. While constructing a bulb with mercury vapor, Case remembered some bulbs containing argon that he had developed for the infrared signaling system. He began experimenting with them:

> I had this bulb hooked up directly with the output of a four stage amplifying system; one terminal going to the heated filament and the other terminal to the grid. The microphone for taking up the voice variations was connected up to the input of the first bulb of the amplifying system through a transformer . . . the new light was heated and the results were most pronounced and pleasing. The voice variation after being transformed into the electrical variations produced a beautiful glow discharge in the argon bulb.[12]

Using a Powers projector modified to serve as a sound camera, Case and Sponable filmed the variations produced by this process and received results superior to anything Case had previously noted:

> I took a piece of film upon which I had photographed the word "hello" and installed this in the camera and passed it by

the slit as near the same speed as we had taken it and by means of the Thalofide Cell on the other side of the slit and an incandescent light held so that it would shine through the film through the slit and onto the Thalofide cell heard the word "hello" reproduced.[13]

They found the solution that had eluded de Forest. This light cell, which Case initially called the helio-light, and later renamed the Aeo light, proved pivotal in successful sound film production.[14]

Almost immediately, Case called his patent attorney, Eugene Thompson of Denison & Thompson in Syracuse. While Case was conferring with Thompson at the lab, de Forest called, requesting some nitrogen-filled tubes and complaining about further troubles with his recording system. Not wanting to reveal what he had just discovered, Case did not mention his breakthrough to de Forest.[15]

That evening, after the patent attorney had given his approval, Case telegrammed de Forest: "CAN YOU TAKE NIGHT TRAIN FOR AUBURN? IMPORTANT DEVELOPMENT." De Forest arrived in

Theodore Case in office of Case Research Lab, circa 1923.

Auburn early on December 15. Case and Sponable showed de Forest the first form of the new cell, and their simple recordings of the word "hello." De Forest immediately asked to take one of the cells back with him, and Case complied.

The next day, John Taber, an Auburn lawyer, soon-to-be U. S. Congressman, and Case's personal attorney, wrote to de Forest, broaching the subject of marketing the cells: "He [Case] desires to prepare to market these devices along with you in such a way as will be best for all concerned."[16] De Forest expressed interest in the possibilities, but claimed the situation still too nebulous to work out a definite agreement. He wanted to conduct a public demonstration, and hoped to get financial backing from Case and his friends as he launched his company.[17]

Case became increasingly distrustful of de Forest, and he worried about proper credit for inventing the gas glow discharge bulb. In lab notes, Case continually noted Sponable's presence during demonstrations, and reaffirmed several times that de Forest had considered a similar idea but did not pursue it:

> Earl I. Sponable was with me during these experiments and assisted me with them. He also heard Dr. De Forest mention the fact that he had tried the tungsten filament, saw him draw the diagram of the tube he used . . . and also heard him say that he had obtained no results by the addition of the filament, saw no advantage in it and dropped it.[18]

The idea for the gas glow light grew out of work on light cells that the lab had pursued since 1916, and out of earlier ideas that Case had explored in college. Case admitted that the idea came back into his head following his contact with de Forest, but adding a coated filament near another electrode and other changes made it work.[19] Case accepted de Forest's suggestions, but also followed his own ideas. Working on these cells, Case's assistants displayed the same patient approach they had exhibited in earlier projects, qualities that de Forest by this time seemed to lack.

By mid-December, work on perfecting the glow lights became the

Case Research Lab's sole focus. Case's staff created and tested light cells, made adjustments to the shape, filament lengths, and coatings, and shipped bulbs to de Forest. In time for the holidays in 1922, Case sent de Forest a bulb by way of a porter on a Pullman sleeping car, accompanied by a piece of film with sound track exclaiming "Merry Christmas."[20]

But who invented the tube? In December, de Forest wrote to Case, suggesting changes to his photion tube, clearly referring to the cell that Case called the helio-light. It made no difference to de Forest that others might question his proprietorship of the invention. By now, de Forest was using the Case Research Lab, officially or unofficially, as his research facility. He continued to make suggestions, including sketches of cell improvements in letters to Case, but de Forest was becoming increasingly involved in the establishment of his sound film company, as his New York studios concentrated on film production and promotion. He was also still

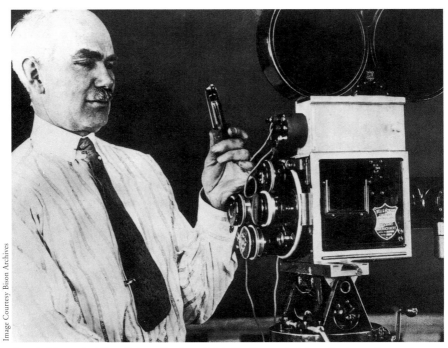

Lee de Forest holding light cell, circa 1923. De Forest holds a photion tube, or Aeo light, depending on one's viewpoint, near a Bell and Howell camera.

involved with De Forest Radio Telephone & Telegraph Company (which he would later sell to help finance the film company). As always, de Forest urged haste:

> Please start on which <u>you</u> think is easiest to make and let me have one as soon as possible. . . . For I yesterday got the finest lines of the clearest reproduction I have <u>ever</u> had, from my Hg-filled photion. I know these with filaments will give much more light, which is all I now lack, for loudness. . . . With these I'm <u>sure</u> I'll have a Happy New Year![21]

On January 9, 1923, Sponable traveled to de Forest's studio to observe his progress and test two recording hookups that had worked at the Case Research Lab but failed to operate properly for de Forest. During this session, de Forest used professional musicians for the first time. In a lengthy notebook entry, Sponable commented on de Forest's system, its positive points, and flaws. He compared different types of microphones and made suggestions for improvements. The entry revealed Sponable's growing knowledge about sound film and his emerging role as a key figure in understanding and developing the system.[22]

During the visit, Sponable and de Forest successfully tried a new Case bulb in which the filament remained unlit while the gas glowed. Sponable returned to Auburn the next day, and reported the tube's success. Case immediately called a meeting with Denison & Thompson to discuss filing another patent application. Throughout January, lab associates continued testing variations to the Aeo light and sending experimental cells to de Forest.

With the problem of the recording catalyst addressed, an adequate microphone became the focus. Again, de Forest tried without success to build a suitable microphone, and he asked Case to design one.[23] To create a microphone for sound film production, Case needed to record performances. Sponable designed a sound camera and had the Precision Machine Company in New York City build it. The lab used the camera to create experimental soundtracks. By February, the Case Research Lab was producing sound recordings daily, experimenting with different cells, microphone technology, and the performer's location in relation to the microphone, recognizing a practical problem of physical space and distance in addition to technical concerns. Local talents of varying levels, including Sponable and Cushman, contributed to these recordings. Even Case participated by playing mandolin.

Near the end of February, Case, Sponable, and Taber visited de Forest in his studio. They were not impressed by his first films of synchronized sound and images. One of them recalled, "In practically all of his music records a bad ground noise was present. This noise was so evident that it was a very objectionable feature. . . . His reproducing system was very weak and inefficient."[24]

During the visit, de Forest asked Case to send the Case Research Lab's recording amplifier to New York, to compare to his own equipment.[25] De Forest knew his product had flaws, and he recognized the superior quality of Case's equipment. De Forest and Case also began discussions about forming a company to commercialize de Forest's sound film system using Case Research Lab inventions.

Egyptian Dancer, segment of one of the first De Forest Phonofilms, 1923.

On March 13, Case attended de Forest's Phonofilm demonstration for members of the New York press and judged the presentation premature. De Forest showed four films. Case rated only one, an Egyptian Dance, "very good." He believed the problems stemmed from de Forest's projector and amplifier, both of which Case had earlier suggested he refine. De Forest was not one to take unsolicited advice, but Case kept trying. "I hope that he will now fix up his projector and also improve his projecting amplifier," Case commented following the Phonofilm demonstration.[26]

In Auburn, Case, Sponable, and Cushman, along with lawyers Thompson and Taber, met to discuss their relationship with de Forest and to revisit the idea of a contract for using Case Research Lab inventions in Phonofilm.[27] During the discussions, Case decided not to invest in de Forest's film company.

Business negotiations began inauspiciously. Taber judged de Forest's initial offers of royalties and modest rental fees unacceptable, because they conveyed little credit for Case's inventions. Taber commented to de Forest:

> Mr. Case feels that having supplied the thalofide cell . . . and having developed the heliolight and the light with oxide coated electrodes, both of which singly and in combination have enabled you to take sound pictures in the most satisfactory manner yet worked out, that some more substantial recognition of his work in connection with the sound pictures should be made than you propose.[28]

De Forest objected to using attorneys in the ensuing discussions. He wrote Case complaining of interference, and suggested that second parties obstructed amicable agreement on contract terms. De Forest also could not understand Case's hesitation:

> I have been working like the devil for over three years, building up a situation which promises to afford a very wide market for the Thallafide [sic] Cell, such a market as no other source offers to you, or will offer for a long time to come. I admire the

Thallafide Cell and certainly want to use it very much in
my work . . .

It is certainly only good business on your part to cooperate with
me to bring the Fonofilm [*sic*] out on to the market at an early
date and in as practical and simple a form as possible . . . I
cannot see why your efforts to improve my Photion Light
would not be well justified.[29]

Case and de Forest clearly had differing views on ownership of the gas
glow discharge tube. Again, de Forest mentioned his photion tube, as if
Case's lab work was a contract service. De Forest knew he needed Case's
inventions to make his system work, and perhaps he felt threatened by
Case's moves to patent his inventions. De Forest candidly raised the specter
of litigation:

As regards the Patent situation at the recording end: I have, as
you know, a broad, basic Patent covering the type of Tube we
are using. So that . . . I am the only one that could employ this
type of Tube. . . . Also, in early applications I have disclosed the
use of Helium Gas for these Photion tubes and have constructed
several Tubes filled with Helium Gas in 1921 . . . I hope that
you and I will never get into an interference dispute in the
Patent Office, but I would have no difficulty in establishing an
early date on the use of Helium. As to the . . . Oxide-coated
Filament, you are unquestionably entitled to broad claims, and I
should very much dislike to have to use a dimly lighted tungsten
filament, as shown in my 1921 Patent Application, although
such I can use if such an arrangement is necessary.[30]

But it was posturing. De Forest's system worked badly with a tungsten
filament bulb. The argumentative "I'll go somewhere else if I have to" tone
was his way to avoid admitting that Case's inventions made Phonofilm
possible. As an excuse for not fully crediting Case's work on gas glow
discharge tube, de Forest urged that the Case Research Lab's role should
remain secret for commercial concerns.[31]

Case privately demonstrated his talking films in his Auburn studio on March 17.[32] The following day, articles covering the progress of talking pictures appeared simultaneously in the *Syracuse Herald* and the *New York Herald*, with very different stories regarding inventors. "Talking Movies Invented by Auburn Man Through Aid of Strong Light Ray," claimed the Syracuse paper. The *New York Herald* trumpeted Lee de Forest's latest invention and achievement, including the role of his photion tube. Case was not mentioned in the latter article.[33]

Agreement on financial issues proved as difficult as credit negotiations. While urging Case to buy stock in Phonofilm, de Forest hedged on committing to royalty agreements, saying with some validity that it was impossible to predict any future success. Case eventually proposed a flat rental charge of $3.50 a week per cell for both the Aeo lights and Thalofide Cells. Distrustful of de Forest, Case wanted a clear-cut deal and "nothing else, no stock, no guarantee, no share of profits either gross or not."[34]

De Forest tried to interest other Auburn investors in the project. Steel accompanied industrialist E. Donaldson Clapp of E. D. Clapp Manufacturing Company to a demonstration at de Forest's studio in March.[35] During the visit, de Forest offered Steel a position with Phonofilm, which he freely admitted to Case. De Forest also tried to offer a carrot to Clapp, by mentioning to Case four vacancies on his board of directors, one of which could be available for Clapp.[36] Clapp did not take the bait and declined to invest in the company, feeling the deal was weighted too heavily in de Forest's favor.[37]

Nov. 25, 1924. 1,517,103

T. W. CASE

PHOTO ELECTRIC CELL

Filed April 26, 1921

Fig 1.

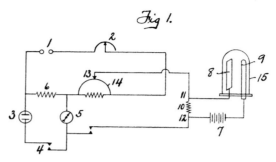

Fig 2.

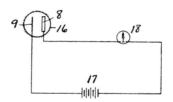

Fig 3.

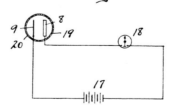

INVENTOR

J.W. Case

BY

Demison Thompson

ATTORNEY

Patent drawing; photo electric cell, filed April 26, 1921.

Chapter 5

De Forest Phonofilm
and the Case Lab

5

De Forest Phonofilm and the Case Lab

On April 4, 1923, Lee de Forest previewed Phonofilm with a lecture and demonstration for the New York Electrical Society and on April 15, De Forest Phonofilm premiered to the public at the Rivoli Theater in New York. Cushman, Sponable, and John Taber attended, and gave the show mixed reviews. A *New York Times* reporter covering the premiere commented that the films lacked synchronized images and human voices.[1] Another audience member remarked less generously that Phonofilm sounded "like an enormous phonograph with its horn stuffed up by a mattress."[2]

Despite the mixed reception, de Forest pressed on. He continued wrangling over contract terms, complaining that Case's rental fees were too steep. De Forest also tried to lure away another Case Lab employee, suggesting to Case that Sponable spend three days a week in the Phonofilm studio.[3] Coupled with his earlier offer to Steel, de Forest's actions were admissions of the Case Research Lab's superior technical expertise.

In April, Taber proposed a lease agreement between de Forest and the Case Research Lab covering use of Thalofide Cells and Aeo lights for sound film purposes only, with manufacturing charges of $100 each for Aeo lights, and $50 each for Thalofide Cells. Rental fees for all cells would be charged on a sliding scale depending on rental price of films, which corresponded with the size of the theater, from $2 to $7. Case required

De Forest Phonofilms truck, circa 1924.

that de Forest rent at least one hundred cells by October 1, 1924, and two hundred the next year. After a few more months of cajoling and excuses, de Forest finally signed the contract and returned it in September.

When Sponable returned to New York City in early May 1923 he found de Forest's studio not yet completely outfitted for producing talking pictures, with incomplete equipment and film that had to be taken out of the studio to be developed. Sponable and de Forest's staff tried several microphones, including a recent Case Research Lab invention called the air-thermo microphone, which Sponable had brought with him. But they couldn't conduct complete tests because wires burnt out due to problems with an amplifier.

Case and his staff continued their own sound film work in Auburn. They further tested the air-thermo microphone, introduced a cover glass on the slit for the recording mechanism in the camera, and explored amplifier arrangements, finally using two Western Electric amplifiers in a series. The test films that used this new arrangement got positive results. Sponable and Steel returned to de Forest's studio with the new amplifier setup and several air-thermo microphones, hoping to solve the difficulties that de Forest's men continued to encounter.[4] Case, already in New York City, joined them. Sponable and Steel also brought their modified camera to compare it with a German camera de Forest's staff was using, and to determine the problem in their recording method. When de Forest, in France, heard of Sponable and Steel's assistance, he expressed gratitude but also admitted unease, because it showed that his men were having trouble in getting the studio up and running.[5]

De Forest also grew aggravated by alterations to the New York studio camera, which delayed production of films he had expected to be shipped to Europe. He sent a perturbed cable to W. E. Waddell, General Manager of his Phonofilm studio.[6] Waddell, not seeking to incur de Forest's wrath, pleaded for Case to intervene. Case, who had earlier expressed reservations about Phonofilm quality, responded to de Forest bluntly:

> Mr. Waddell wished me to write you concerning the altering of the camera. When I went down to your Studio to start the set, I found . . . considerable jerkiness both in the taking camera and reproducing projector there. I brought my own camera down to check this, as we have perfectly smooth motion. I obtained perfect piano and voice films on mine, but could not get anything that was good enough to show on your camera. I therefore recommended that they fix the mechanical end before trying to produce anything, as there would be no more quicker way to kill this proposition than to put out bad stuff.[7]

Sponable began regularly visiting de Forest's studio, advising on all areas of the sound film recording process.[8] During this time, Case began trying to interest Western Electric Company in the thermo microphone, while de Forest and his representatives spent substantial time in Europe trying to cultivate overseas interest in their product.

As work on Phonofilm progressed, the press continued to marvel at Lee de Forest's new invention. Articles in *The World*, *Scientific American* and *The Evening World Radio* between January and April 1923 covered at length the talking pictures of the radio wizard. Each time, the Case Research Lab gained mention only for the Thalofide Cell. Case fired back by having another article appear in the *Auburn Citizen* in September, a brief of which *Citizen* Managing Editor William O. Dapping sent to the Associated Press, to ensure that it would appear in newspapers throughout the United States.[9] The article had one intended purpose. "If de Forest kicks again," Dapping wrote to Case, "tell him we consider that Auburn is the home of the new invention."[10]

In September, Sponable visited Western Electric's laboratories, where he discussed production of a specialized transformer and conducted tests with the thermo microphone. Twice during the remainder of the month Sponable returned to de Forest's studio with microphones and improved amplifiers. The extent to which Sponable had become responsible for Phonofilm's sound system was reflected in a later journal entry, written following a trip to de Forest's studio. Sponable took another microphone to New York for testing, and "showed them [de Forest's staff] [the] method of making up elements. Rewired their amplifiers; set up our special camera; [and] showed where their projector was mechanically incorrect giving them roughness in the film."[11]

While Sponable retooled de Forest's equipment, Case became involved in negotiations for use of Case Research Lab inventions by De Forest Phonofilms Limited, the British branch of the Phonofilm venture. De Forest referred Case to C. H. Elwell, the head of British operations. Elwell, via de Forest, begged Case not to lend or sell any more of his Thalofide Cells to European competitors, especially Gaumont Studios in Paris, to whom Case had sent a Thalofide Cell earlier in 1923.[12]

By October, de Forest had twenty-five talking pictures ready for public release. By November, he arranged for Phonofilm productions to be shown in two Keith Company theaters, one in Mt. Vernon, New York, and the other in Cleveland, Ohio. De Forest promised no lack of showmanship and advertising to assure Phonofilm's success, because public reception would determine the length of their stay in each venue.[13] De Forest also mentioned to Case that motion picture rather than vaudeville audiences should be their target.

In December, de Forest demonstrated the thermo-microphone to the press, and again Case's contribution was minimalized. Perturbed, Case wrote to de Forest concerning a *New York Times* article that stated the original microphone idea was de Forest's. In letters, and in a phone conversation overheard by Cushman, de Forest assured Case that the Case Research Lab had "full and proper credit" for the invention.[14]

In January 1924, Sponable visited Western Electric's laboratory to again test the thermo microphone. He then stopped by de Forest's studio, where he heard a Phonofilm recording that he considered "the best record so far by the Phonofilm people."[15] Sponable's repeated trips between Auburn and New York City were finally beginning to show results, although Phonofilm quality continued to vary.

Later that month, Case, Cushman, and Sponable returned to New York with a carload of equipment to set up in de Forest's studio. Case pointed out problems to de Forest's staff and tried to impress upon them that they needed to "do their best to correct the present stuff."[16] Continual technical problems were perhaps due to a lack of quality among technicians on de Forest's staff or lack of supervision due to de Forest's spending extended periods away from his studio.

Case repeatedly admonished de Forest about product quality, but by early 1924 it became obvious to Case that in de Forest's mind quality ranked second to promotion. That resulted in a fateful decision: when Case, Sponable, and Cushman returned from the January trip, following yet another round of suggesting improvement they knew would not be followed, they decided to build their own camera for making sound pictures.[17] From then on, Case worked toward perfecting his own sound-on-film system while simultaneously collaborating with de Forest and providing Phonofilm with Aeo lights, Thalofide Cells, and technical support.

Case purchased a new Bell & Howell camera, and Sponable pursued designing an appropriate sound head for synchronized recording of sound and images. He took the camera to the Simplex shop of Precision Machine Company in New York City, and consulted with their technicians about possible alterations. Cushman talked to Bausch & Lomb representatives about lenses and another company about motors. Sponable met with Bell & Howell representatives in Chicago, where they worked out thirteen alterations needed to outfit the experimental camera.[18] Lab assistants also ordered a Simplex projector, to remodel to their specifications at the lab.

Lab assistants constructed a small room in the lab basement to serve as a recording studio. They deadened sound with hair felt walls, brought in lights, and hung a cheap curtain for a background. "I do not think we need a plush curtain at present," the frugal Sponable admonished.[19] He also warned that the room would get very hot in the summer, and suggested that the Case Research Lab consider assembling a more complete studio if it wanted to produce pictures.

In January, de Forest gave Case an enthusiastic progress report on his Phonofilm production, *Abraham Lincoln Episodes*, and he invited Case to New York to view it. But after a February showing of the Lincoln film, *New York Herald* columnist Robert Sherwood remarked that, while they were the best talking movies so far:

> Phonofilm still leaves much to be desired. The sound is so vastly less realistic than the pictures themselves that it can scarcely carry conviction. It is inordinately loud, and its tonal quality is that of a radio receiving set on a night when there is a great deal of static . . . When Lincoln concluded the Gettysburg Address, one instinctively waited for the announcer to say 'Station WJZ broadcasting—stand by for Uncle Wiggly's bedtime story.'[20]

Credit continued to be an issue between Case and de Forest. Following further debate, Case finally got what he wanted, admission in writing of his role in Phonofilm's development. Judging from Phonofilm's public reception, it was a dubious honor. De Forest wrote:

> Confirming our conversation I cheerfully agree, in considera-tion of the fact that so many of the devices and methods we are using in the Phonofilm are of your design or improvement, to

use the terms De Forest-Case System or De Forest-Case on all
our literature and advertising, or wherever the system is
mentioned so far as it is in our power to control.[21]

Despite promises, by the end of February, Case and de Forest again
verbally sparred over credit following a theater director's refusal to change
the electric marquee at the Rivoli to read "De Forest-Case Phonofilm."
Rivoli Director Hugo Riesenfeld, a long-time de Forest supporter, argued
that a name change would confuse the public. Riesenfeld also declined to
run an article in the program giving Case partial credit for the invention.
De Forest professed dismay at the situation, but added such a position was
"a natural one to take on their [the theater owner's] part."[22] Financial
problems also arose, and the Case Research Lab billed Phonofilm for
several unpaid invoices from seven months previous.

Through the spring and summer of 1924, Case and his staff continued
working on the sound camera and projector. While Case vacationed in
Saint Augustine, Florida, and Pinehurst, South Carolina, he and Sponable
corresponded regularly, discussing technical issues, reporting on camera
progress, and exchanging news—including the latest personnel resigning
from Phonofilm. Sponable updated Case about construction of a sound-
proof camera booth needed for film production. The booth, made of hair
felt and double balsa wood walls (materials with good sound deadening
qualities), enclosed the camera and cameraman. Sponable also traveled to
Bell & Howell and General Electric to discuss problems and developments
with the lab's sound film system.

In June, de Forest made an agreement with Famous Players-Lasky
Corporation to install Phonofilms apparatus in theaters in twenty-seven
cities across the United States. Several Central New York theater owners also
expressed interest in Phonofilm. John Breslin of Auburn's Universal Theater
wrote to de Forest requesting a Phonofilm exhibition. De Forest referred the
request to Case, saying the theater could not afford to pay very much, and
that he would leave the decision to Case. In June, Case approached Waddell
about installing Phonofilm in a six-theater chain across upstate New York,

DE FOREST PHONOFILMS, INC.

220 WEST 42ND STREET

NEW YORK

LEE de FOREST, PRESIDENT   TELEPHONES: CHICKERING 0620
                                                                0621

February 11th, 1924.

Mr. T.W.Case,
Auburn,
N.Y.

Dear Mr. Case:

Confirming our conversation I cheerfully agree, in consideration of the fact that so many of the devices and methods we are using in the Phonofilm are of your design or improvement, to use the terms DeForest-Case System or DeForest-Case on all our literature and advertising, or wherever the system is mentioned so far as it is in our power to control.

Very truly yours,

Lee de Forest

LdeF/H

The letter from Lee de Forest to Theodore Case, affirming Case credit for work on Phonofilm, February 11, 1924.

including venues in Rome, Oneida, and Canastota. When Phonofilms premiered in Auburn, they were enthusiastically received. De Forest himself attended a private screening at the Universal.[23]

Advertisement for coming features at Auburn's Universal Theater, June 7, 1924, highlighting the "8th Wonder of the World," Theodore Case's talking moving pictures.

In response to Case's suggestion of showing Phonofilms in upstate New York, de Forest asked him to finance the equipment and installation of these theaters.[24] The request soon extended to theaters throughout the eastern United States. Case agreed to fund up to fifteen theaters at a time, out of his own pocket, at the cost of a $1000 loan per theater to De Forest Phonofilm. The Case Research Lab would receive all box office receipts until the sum was paid off. De Forest also asked Case to handle the installations, but Case declined, saying his staff was too small to act as theater crews. By the end of the month, Case financed the installation of equipment in theaters in Boston and St. Louis.[25]

In early July, Phonofilms enjoyed a successful showing at the McVickers Theater in Chicago. That same month, de Forest sent Case an inventory list of Thalofide cells being used in theaters, and the list included venues in New York and Brooklyn, as well as theaters in Providence, Philadelphia, Auburn, and Cleveland. Despite some positive response, the numbers did not add up to a spectacular success. De Forest still dreamed of revolutionizing the film industry, but he was not having much impact.

In July, Case proposed to de Forest that he produce Phonofilms in Auburn. De Forest granted permission:

> The Phonofilm Corporation will agree to your installing the
> necessary equipment in your proposed studio in Auburn, and to

your . . . making of such Phonofilms as you can . . . in that
location, selecting . . . numbers which you believe the theaters
will demand. The Phonofilm Corporation will purchase . . .
prints of all such numbers as far as we can place them with
exhibitors, and pay you 50% of the amounts received.[26]

De Forest would not finance experimentation however, or production
costs for films that Phonofilm Corporation did not purchase. Case also
began investigating a licensing agreement with Western Electric for commercial use of amplifiers. When Kenesaw Mountain Landis, a Chicago native,
visited Auburn, he was filmed by the Case Lab, and Case's brother-in-law
Dwight Eldred, who had joined the lab staff as business manager, offered de
Forest the picture for the McVickers Theater in Chicago.[27]

On July 25, Phonofilm Manager Waddell arranged to film President
Calvin Coolidge and Senator Robert "Fighting Bob" LaFollette in
Washington D.C. Coolidge, running for re-election, faced Democratic
challenger John W. Davis, and LaFollette, a Wisconsin senator and third-
party Progressive candidate. De Forest wrote to Case, asking him to have

Filming Senator LaFollette in Washington D.C., 1924. Notice that the equipment in
the foreground has Case Research Lab stamped on it.

his camera ready on a day's notice. Ever concerned with others stealing Phonofilm's technology, de Forest urged secrecy regarding the project. Case agreed to do the recording, and by August 8, he and his men assembled the equipment, including the modified Bell & Howell camera, amplifiers, Aeo lights, microphones, and other materials, and loaded it into their Studebaker. Cushman and Sponable drove the car to Washington while Case and Eldred followed by train.[28]

On the morning of August 11, Case and Sponable met de Forest and his cameraman, Mr. Blakely, and began setting up the equipment on the White House lawn, debating the best location for filming. According to Case, "one of the outstanding features [of the morning's activities] was that nobody seemed to know anything definite."[29] When cameras were ready, and shade umbrellas acquired at some trouble, T. L. Townsend of National Electric Supply Company invited the party to attend lunch at the City Club. Case, Sponable, and Blakely stayed behind, not wishing to leave the equipment unattended. At around 1:30 PM, President Coolidge unexpectedly emerged from the White House. Sponable recalled:

> President Coolidge appeared dressed in a light gray suit, walking towards our apparatus with Mrs. Coolidge and their son, John at some distance in the rear and the usual number of secret service men trailing. The President did not appear to be in a particularly friendly mood and his first words were, "I don't see why you people do not do as you agreed to and set up on the porch," to which Mr. Case rather meekly responded that he did not know the apparatus was to be placed on the porch.[30]

Case, an ardent Republican, was taken aback by the President's demeanor. "It was not exactly the words" he recalled, "but the manner in which he said them [that] dumb-founded me . . . I . . . expected to see a courteous man. I was so taken back by his looks, manner and deportment that I was at a loss to say anything for a while."[31] Case offered to move the equipment anywhere more to Coolidge's liking and encouraged the

President to look through the finder on the camera. Coolidge peered through but gave Case little response, only mumbling a few comments before heading back inside the White House.

Case's impressions clearly betrayed his social standing and political inclinations. He was shocked that Coolidge, a prosperous Republican like himself, could be so rude. As a man of science, Case was also dismayed that the President showed no interest in the technology:

> I should have thought that anyone would have showed some slight interest in an entirely new apparatus for which they were about to perform. I had intended asking if Mrs. Coolidge might not like to be Phonofilmed and that I would present the film to her for her private use but after this I decided to stick to business and depart as it was the most frigid, hot day I had ever seen.[32]

Coolidge reappeared about ten minutes later, in a new suit and with speech in hand. He brusquely asked who was running the show, and de

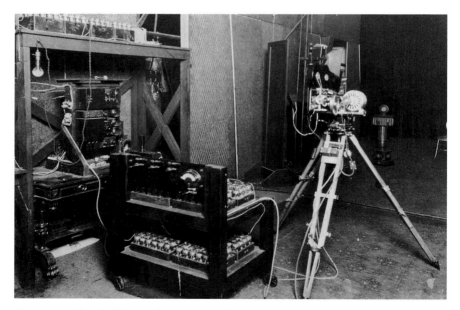

Case Research Lab, film studio in carriage house, circa 1924.

Forest immediately jumped in to take the lead. Case deferred without hesitation. The camera crew conducted a sound test before recording the speech, and Case had to ask Coolidge to speak up—his low tone did not register well for the recording equipment. Then, with Sponable instead of Blakely behind the Case Research Lab's modified camera, Case gave the signal for Coolidge to begin. The President, supposedly prepared to give a three-minute speech, spoke for much longer, and he became annoyed when he had to stop when the camera ran out of film. De Forest hastily explained the delay to the President, and Case assured him they could overlap the film after putting on a new magazine. After the momentary delay, recording continued. When they finished, Coolidge, without much civility "turned on his heel and walked straight into the White House."[33]

The film crew then headed to find Senator La Follette at the Capitol building. Despite original plans to film LaFollette the following day, Case informed de Forest they would be filming the Senator immediately, as he "was not going to stay in Washington another hot day."[34] Coolidge's brusque treatment of the film crew, as well as the muggy weather, probably played into Case's snappish actions. While trying to track down LaFollette, the film team set up on the Capitol steps, after arguing with the Capitol guards over permission to film at that location. A crowd gathered, and finally LaFollette appeared. Case's politics and views of social graces again faced reevaluation, as LaFollette "immediately won the respect of all present by his genial and fiery manner."[35] In contrast to Coolidge, Case recalled that LaFollette:

> was just as nice as he could possibly be and wanted to know all about the apparatus and wanted to know what he was to do . . . was as likeable a person as President Coolidge was the opposite. Of course, I do not agree with LaFollette's ideas or the way he acted during the war but as for being a thorough gentleman and extremely likeable there is no question.[36]

With an audience to cheer him on, LaFollette gave an old-fashioned fire-and-brimstone performance, complete with enthusiasm and gestures.

LaFollette's voice was much more powerful than Coolidge's, and after the first take the film crew shot another, adjusting the amplification to better match with the tenor of his voice. LaFollette gladly obliged, and when finished, he graciously posed for photographers.

Recording done, Case and Sponable drove the Studebaker to New York, while Cushman returned to Auburn to develop the second version of LaFollette's speech. De Forest, Eldred, and Blakely carried the rest of the film to New York by train. In all, despite the heat, confusion, and testy temperaments, Case rated the trip a success. Understanding the importance of what they were doing—these brief talking movies were the first sound film appearance of a United States President—and perhaps not without a touch of vanity, Case recorded in his notes that copies of the Coolidge and LaFollette films would be given to the Smithsonian Institution.[37]

Phonofilm continued to make marginal progress. In August, de Forest asked Case for $5000 more to outfit theaters in Syracuse, New York, Pottsville, Pennsylvania, and three venues in New Jersey. De Forest also approached Bell & Howell about buying a camera identical to the Case Research Lab's experimental model, which had worked so successfully during the Washington trip. After contacting Case for his permission to fulfill de Forest's request, Bell & Howell proceeded to make the camera for de Forest. But the company told him that in the future, he would have to pay pro-rated development charges to the Case Research Lab for modifications (the camera had cost Case $6,047 to build, more than half of which was development costs).[38]

Increasingly cracks appeared in the tenuous Case-de Forest relationship. Again Case questioned the quality of de Forest's product in his inability to sell contracts in large cities, and complained of a continuing lack of credit lines in presentations. De Forest Phonofilm consistently lagged in its installation loan payments, rental fees and other invoices. At the end of August, Eldred informed de Forest that, in addition to overdue invoices, the October 1 deadline for a minimum purchase of cells was fast approaching. Phonofilm was far from meeting its contract agreement. In short, de Forest owed the Case Research Lab $6500.[39]

Claims of hardship by de Forest's staff failed to elicit sympathy. "This is almost our entire revenue from you this year," Eldred wrote, "and it handicaps you at this time not because the contract is unjust but because of lack of capital. You haven't been able to develop this past year as fast as you expected to."[40] De Forest pleaded for a six-month extension. He admitted that Phonofilm development was behind schedule, but tried to paint a rosy picture, forecasting more theaters and installments happening with increasing frequency in the coming months. But, positive predictions aside, it would be "a very severe hardship to pay you [by] October 1 the minimum amount called for in the contract."[41] Case requested that de Forest come to Auburn to discuss the situation with Taber, or the October deadline would stand.

When the Coolidge Phonofilm appeared in public, the Case Research Lab again failed to receive credit. Case did not take the slight lightly, especially since the bills were piling up. He demanded credit from de Forest:

> Seeing that we made up a special portable apparatus to take President Coolidge and La Follette's pictures, that we took it with a camera of our own design and that we used a new type of Aeo light and different circuit arrangements and that your camera man could not have taken the picture if he had wanted to as there are certain technical adjustments on our design camera which he knew nothing about or you either. . . . I wish to call your attention that . . . this title [Taken by Case Studios] be incorporated with the film. . . . You give excuses that the theater owner would not accept such titles. . . . I have heard this line of argument before and wish you to distinctly understand that this time I will not accept any excuses.[42]

By September's end, de Forest had rented only twenty-three of the required fifty Thalofide Cells for the October deadline. Case's staff packed the remaining twenty-seven cells and told de Forest they were being sent. At one point, de Forest even begged for a price reduction on a single cell, claiming that one of his employees, Blakely (the cameraman on the Coolidge trip), had ruined it by failing to turn off a switch. Blakely made

"Oh Mister Gallagher and Mister Shean," sheet music for the popular song by vaudeville duo Gallagher and Shean, who appeared before Case's camera in the fall of 1924. Sheet music in the collection of the Cayuga Museum.

only $100 a week, de Forest whined, and it would be a hardship for him to pay for the cell. That's between you and your employee, Case replied. Eventually Case accepted partial payment, but he demanded the balance by November 15, sarcastically reminding de Forest that he, too, had bills to pay.[43]

Near the end of September 1924, Case and Sponable filmed popular vaudeville performers Ed Gallagher and Al Shean, along with Fifi D'Orsay, who were appearing at Wieting Opera House in nearby Syracuse. Finding the basement recording studio insufficient, Case had moved his recording equipment to the second floor of the estate carriage house and converted it into a sound studio.

While rental checks dribbled in, Case and de Forest argued over a damaged copy of the Coolidge film and squabbled over Elwell's order for a Bell & Howell camera for Phonofilm's British operations without using de Forest as a middleman. In October, de Forest still owed money. "The difference between the number of weeks due and the number of weeks paid leaves two thousand thirty-seven weeks at $2.00 a week to fulfill minimum requirements for the year," wrote Eldred. "If this is correct . . . you owe us $4074.00 for unpaid rentals to October 1, 1924, and payable October 15, 1924."[44]

Mechanical and promotional problems with Phonofilm installations at

Advertisement for the National Theater in Richmond, Virginia, late 1924, promoting the showing of De Forest Phonofilms.

two Syracuse theaters, the Empire and the Rivoli, created a headache for Case and made him further question de Forest's methods. The theaters fought over the order in which films were sent to them, and the lack of a three-week gap between first and second runs. The Empire had continual problems with focus and amplification. Case and Sponable spent time in Syracuse trying to correct the technical problems, but could do nothing about the squabbling theater owners. The final straw came when the Rivoli began showing the Coolidge film on the last day that the Empire had it. "The whole operation is being run so poorly that I am sick of it," wrote Case angrily. "I have never seen anything so mismanaged or bungled in my life."[45] De Forest Phonofilm ended up canceling the Rivoli contract, and Waddell begged for Case's understanding. "You must try and be a little more patient with us," Waddell wrote, admitting that the operation started too quickly and expanded without adequate planning.[46]

By the end of October, de Forest still couldn't pay off Case's loans for theater installations and his company continued to fall behind in rental fees. Case threatened to cancel the agreement, and demanded the bulk of payment in frustration. De Forest tried to use a deal to distribute Phonofilms in Canada as a means of meeting minimum cell requirements, but quickly fell behind in those payments as well. When de Forest asked for a reduction in Aeo light costs, Case refused, stating that the fees were how the Case Research Lab recovered development costs for their Phonofilm work.[47]

In November, de Forest tried to extend his payments by sending Case a thirty-day note. Case returned it, refusing to grant leniency. He had collected newspaper clippings that mentioned Phonofilm throughout 1924, and he knew that de Forest had not lived up to his agreement to credit Case for his role in Phonofilm development. Case had no faith left in de Forest's word, nor in his ability to pay bills. By late 1924, Case stopped funding theater installations and limited De Forest Phonofilm to the strict specifications of the original contract for light cells.[48]

Advertisement for Loew's Aldine—Premiere of Phonofilms in Pittsburgh, Pennsylvania, October 12, 1924.

When Sponable tested the Gallagher and Shean film at the Rialto in

New York, he said it did not sound good, and criticized the Phonofilm sound reproduction. Waddell tried to assure Case that under normal conditions, the film could be released. But Case worried that the vaudevillians' heavy accents would be difficult to understand if theater sound quality was not perfect. And although de Forest offered to distribute it, he had tried to delay payment for the film until he received payment from theaters for showing it. "Let Mr. Sponable bring it down so that we can run it at the Rivoli Theater some night." Waddell urged.[49] But Case declined, possibly because he and his men were busy making other connections. Sponable had been to see Edward Craft in the engineering department at Western Electric, and Craft gave verbal permission to the Case Research Lab to use Western Electric amplifiers for commercial purposes when and if they had their own system ready.[50]

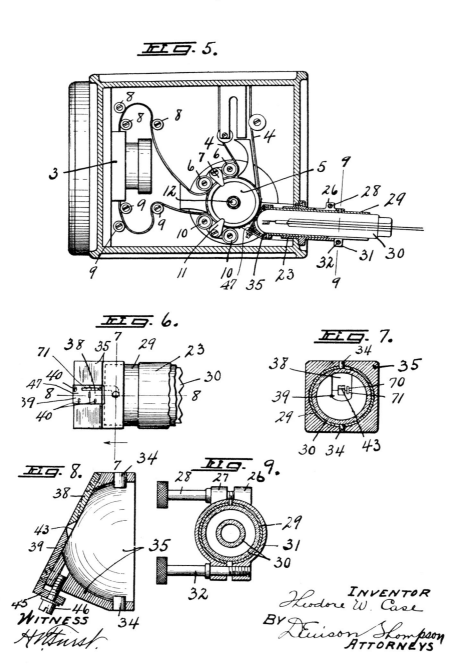

Patent drawing, camera, filed August 22, 1924.

Chapter 6

The End of the Line

6

The End of the Line

De Forest and Case continued collaborating uneasily in early 1925, while Case and his men pursued their own sound film system. To augment the team of Cushman, Sponable, and Steel, Case added another assistant, Pennington Sefton, to his technical staff. In the converted carriage house sound studio, they shot test films using local and imported talent. Musicians, vaudevillians, academics, and relatives appeared before their camera.

Production didn't always run smoothly. After Case filmed several young

singers from the Eastman School of Music, one of them demanded more money, complaining the experience had been "trying, and more difficult than singing an entire concert." She told her advisors that she sang all morning. Nonsense, came the reply, she sang a few numbers before lunch.[1]

Other personalities captured on test films included "the James Boys," a jazz band formed by Paul Whiteman that was appearing in the touring musical *Little Jessie James* at the Grand Theater in Auburn. Noted prison

Test film segment, students from Eastman School of Music, early 1925.

Test film segment of a jazz band, possibly "the James Boys," early 1925.

reformer T. M. Osborne appeared before Case's camera discussing his prison rehabilitation philosophies. Vaudevillian Gus Vesser demonstrated his questionable talents with a singing duck. Musicians included harpists, ukulele players, and the Liberty Quartet, a popular regional singing group. Case's filming activities were often covered in the local paper, and several of the shorts ran at the Grand Theater.

Production work at de Forest's studio had halted. Without Case's money to at least back installation costs, finances became increasingly precarious, and de Forest spent early 1925 soliciting funds. By March, Phonofilm had produced no additional shorts, and new theater contracts stalled without fresh material to offer. To get things moving, Case arranged for private financing with the New York investment firm Hayden, Stone & Company, but de Forest declined, instead choosing to finance Phonofilm via a public sale of stock. "It is a great satisfaction to me, . . . " wrote de Forest, "to know that the public is my partner instead of a bunch of Wall Street bankers, whom I would have to watch day and night to prevent them from taking the proposition away from me as soon as it became really valuable."[2]

De Forest set up Phonofilm Sales Company as the vehicle for handling stock transactions. He published a fifteen-page prospectus, complete with testimonials, accolades from the press, and flattering comments from theater owners—namely one Hugo Riesenfeld. The prospectus lauded Phonofilm as de Forest's crowning achievement, and urged support for "one of the most attractive speculative investments ever offered to the public."[3] When asked what he thought of de Forest's stock selling, Case replied caustically, "I had the whole thing financed by men who could afford to gamble, but he . . . instead went after a lot of poor people who could scarcely afford to lose what they put in. I do not think I need to express my opinion on this matter as it might not get through the mails."[4]

British Phonofilm began shooting pictures in 1925, using a camera of the Case Research Lab's design, and Elwell consistently sought Case's rather than de Forest's advice. When Elwell asked for news

Lee de Forest in Phonofilm studio, circa 1925. This image appeared in Phonofilm Sales Company's stock prospectus.

of the doctor, Case, who was not above reveling in de Forest's financial woes, replied, "Dr. de Forest is not doing much in this country in the way of show. He is busy at present trying to raise money . . . "[5] Elwell requested a man to come to England for a month to help correct problems, but Case couldn't spare Sponable because of the increasing workload in Auburn.

The informal dance with Western Electric continued. In April, a Western Electric representative came to Auburn to discuss amplifier problems. During a May vacation, Case visited Western Electric's headquarters, where talk included work on sound pictures. De Forest knew some of these meetings were taking place, but when he repeatedly asked Case what transpired, Case simply replied, "I did not ask them anything . . . "[6] Going it alone had certainly entered Case's mind by this time, as he wrote to Sponable, "His [de Forest's] stuff is so rotten we can make lots of money . . . if we make good films to show. There is no possible comparison."[7] The potential for patent conflict also occurred to him. While on vacation, Case pondered ways to steer clear of de Forest's patent on the gas discharge tube.

He wrote Sponable with instructions for possible solutions. Sponable, meanwhile, expressed his own growing frustration with de Forest's inability to master the technology:

> De Forest is having much trouble with Aeo lights. He claims they sputter and spoil his records. I have selected them very carefully for him . . . you know our records have practically never been spoiled even when the light did change. His recording must be badly off . . . [8]

By May, the Phonofilm stock-selling scheme ran into trouble. De Forest had hired James W. Elliot as President of Phonofilm Sales Company. Elliot, previously indicted and later cleared on fraudulent stock-selling charges, almost immediately began using the Coolidge Phonofilm as bait in his sales pitch to potential investors. He hired three hundred aggressive salesmen to sell almost $900,000 in securities, and gave each of them copies of the Coolidge film. This action quickly caught the attention of the White House—Coolidge was decidedly unhappy about his image being used for such commercial purposes. The White House ordered the Department of Justice to investigate the reports, and the New York State Attorney General's office seized the books of Phonofilm Sales Company and De Forest Phonofilm Corporation, subpoenaed employees, and ordered the Coolidge film withdrawn from demonstrations to prospective stock buyers. De Forest was not indicted, and he publicly stated that Phonofilm had no connection to the sales company, although they shared an address at 45 West 45th Street.[9]

In June, the Case Research Lab exhibited Phonofilms and other lab inventions in Auburn at the Exposition of Progress, an industrial fair held on the grounds of Auburn Theological Seminary. Local community leaders designed the Exposition as a showcase and celebration of invention and innovation among Auburn industries.[10] The Case Research Lab erected a tent as an impromptu screening room, and offered daily viewings of Phonofilm and Case Research Lab test films, including shorts of the "James Boys," R. H. Hole singing "Mandalay," and T. M. Osborne.

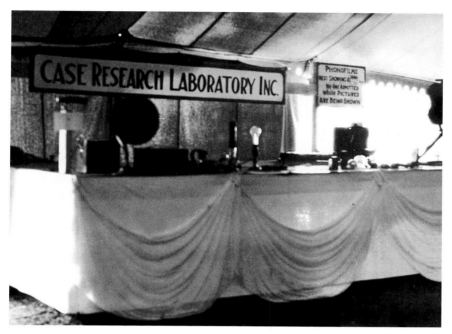

Case Research Lab exhibit, Exposition of Progress, 1925.

Case Research Lab exhibit, film tent, Exposition of Progress, 1925.

Audiences responded enthusiastically, especially during the
evening hours. At one of the
showings, crowds actually
stormed the doors to the tent.
Case's men also assembled a
booth to exhibit other lab
inventions, and they set up
the infrared system with a
beam projecting across the
room, so visitors could see
how it was used in sending
signals. Phonofilm Manager
Waddell visited Auburn

Case Research Lab exhibit, behind the scenes,
Exposition of Progress, 1925.

during the Exposition to see the Case Research Lab's show.

Meanwhile, work at British Phonofilm progressed slowly. Elwell heard
Tri-Ergon's sound film system during a trip to Germany, and freely
admitted that its music reproduction was far superior to de Forest's.[11] By
July, British Phonofilm equipped its first theater for sound. Case continued

Case Research Lab exhibit, Case taking a break
between shows, Exposition of Progress, 1925.

to give Elwell advice,
cautioning him to avoid
the mistakes plaguing de
Forest. During a trip
overseas, Pennington
Sefton visited Elwell. In a
humorous note, Sefton
avoided paying duty on
two light cells he was
delivering by putting
them in his socks. Sefton
reported to Case that

production facilities for British Phonofilm left something to be desired.
The studio in Clopham, he wrote, was "in a rotten old building which

runs all over the place and looks fit for crows nests."[12] But Elwell, who not coincidentally was also working on his own sound film system, did not seem discouraged.

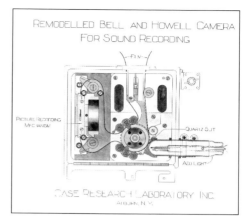

Remodeled Bell and Howell Camera for sound recording, 1925.

By the fall of 1925 de Forest, who had abandoned his own technology when he received the Bell and Howell camera, resumed making pictures. He also experimented with colored film, although the sound quality was poor. The lack of film production through most of 1925 meant that Phonofilm had rented few light cells, and reports to the Case Research Lab for May, June, July, and August were blank. Phonofilm had many light cells left to rent by October. In August, the Case Research Lab prepared to make 300 Thalofide cells to fill Phonofilm's quota for the year.

Case and Sponable continued work on their sound film system. Not satisfied with the sound camera, they sent it back to Bell & Howell for reconstruction. When the camera was returned in September, it still did not operate smoothly enough. Realizing that Bell & Howell had done as much as it could, Case began searching for a local machinist to do precision work. He finally decided upon John M. Wall at Doyle & Wall in Syracuse. Although it was the first construction work Wall had ever done on a camera, he seemed to understand exactly what the lab needed. By the end the month, he had the camera working better than ever before.[13] Sponable, meanwhile, created and supervised the construction of the Case Research Lab's first sound reproducing attachment for projectors. The resulting design moved the sound apparatus below the projection head, ostensibly improving upon the existing technology but also ensuring that previously made sound films, some of which Sponable called "quite bad," could not be played.[14]

While the camera had been nearly perfected, the same could not be said of Case and de Forest's working relationship. Through the summer months, it continued to deteriorate, and Case's business manager began to explore legal action. In early September, Eldred visited former Auburnian and rising lawyer John Foster Dulles in his New York office to discuss possibly breaking the de Forest contract. Case further explained his position to Dulles:

> There are certain reasons why we wish to divorce ourselves from the De Forest Company at the present time. We do not like the way that they have handled matters from a financial standpoint, nor do we like the way they have handled it from a scientific standpoint as we strongly feel the apparatus as we have developed it here is ready to use commercially but as they are handling it we consider it a miserable failure. We are, therefore, sending them a letter . . . informing them of the fact that we terminate the contract. This may produce a situation in which we may be able to clean up their organization by suggesting certain changes and thereby save many stockholders from losing everything.[15]

Dulles affirmed that the contract could be terminated. But he queried whether Case really wanted to take such extreme action rather than renegotiate. Eldred had admitted to Dulles that de Forest could eventually minimize his reliance on Case's products, turning to less expensive and less satisfactory equipment that could produce a crudely working system. Was it better to try and make the existing relationship with de Forest work or go it alone? Despite Dulles' admonishment, Case initially refused to renegotiate unless the terms included reorganization of De Forest Phonofilm. His primary concerns should the deal be broken were the return of his equipment and the strength of his position in any lawsuit.

On September 25, 1925, Case informed de Forest that the contract was terminated because Phonofilm had failed to comply with the terms outlined for light cell quotas and theater installations.[16] Four days later, Phonofilm lawyer George Compton came to Auburn to explore possible renegotiation terms. Case and Sponable showed their films to Compton, who admitted that they were better than anything done at de Forest's studio.[17] Compton requested that Phonofilm board member Benjamin Castle come to Auburn, and before long another board member, Harold Bolster (who had been corresponding with Case since August), also visited the Case Lab.

Castle and Bolster came away impressed with both Case's invention and his hospitality. Castle called the trip to Auburn, "one of the bright spots in the life of a tired businessman."[18] Case and Sponable told Bolster and Castle of their continual problems, and the reasons behind their refusal to continue work with Phonofilm. They would accept no new contract:

> Unless they [Phonofilm management] were able to subordinate De Forest in the organization to such an extent that the management of the company would be taken from his hands and solely under the direction of some other able men. We further advised them that we would not consider any new terms until . . . their present troubles had been permanently dismissed from the Attorney General's office.[19]

Compton and Castle returned to New York with Case's proposal for a new contract: a minimum $3,000 monthly the first year, and $3,600 monthly after that, with minimums figured against 4 percent gross earnings of Phonofilm. A few days later, two more Phonofilm board members, Augustus Thomas and William Elliot, visited Auburn, viewed films, and discussed future possibilities. Again, they expressed enthusiasm at the quality of the work but reservations at de Forest approving any proposal.

Eldred and Dulles drafted a written version of the new contract proposal and forwarded it to Phonofilm. Despite earlier enthusiasm, Phonofilm board members, serving as mouthpieces for de Forest, reported back that they felt they could find cheaper products to use in the system. Eldred remained in New York, further negotiating with Compton and Bolster. They decided that Case should join the discussions.

Eldred wrote to Dulles before the meeting, explaining that he and Case would be in New York to negotiate. They would stand on the terms they originally offered, and expect a contract or they were through with Phonofilm. If de Forest responded negatively, they were prepared to remove their equipment from the Phonofilm studio. But, Eldred asked Dulles, what should we do if Phonofilm refuses to allow such action? By telegram Dulles told Case to bring his de Forest correspondence with him.[20]

The dance continued through October and November, Phonofilm's board members being decidedly more amenable than de Forest to reaching an agreement. In October, the Phonofilm board sent de Forest and Bolster to Auburn to discuss things with Case. At the end of the month, de Forest again proposed new terms, which Case refused. While negotiations continued, the Case Research Lab continued to provide cells, and Case spent time trying to track down several good projectionists for Phonofilm.

In negotiations at the Yale Club, Case, Eldred, Dulles, and Phonofilm board members agreed on a proposal they believed equitable to both parties. But discussions again stalled when de Forest became involved, still arguing that other cells on the market cost less, although they might not be as good. De Forest offered Case stock in Phonofilm rather that a percentage of the gross. Case refused the offer. Several Phonofilm board members went to Dulles' office proposing to reduce the gross percentage to 2 percent and cut the minimum in half. Unacceptable, Dulles replied. Bolster called back later that afternoon with an offer to pay directly a minimum that could be broken up into smaller sums, so that one large payment to the Case Research Lab would not appear on the Phonofilm books. Case said no and counteroffered.[21]

At one point it seemed things were settled. But on November 21, de Forest wrote Case that his patents for the photographic slit and glass cover slit wouldn't stand, and that De Forest Phonofilm would be using other light cells:

> In view of these facts, there will not be the slightest justification
> for me to recommend to the Board of Directors that they now

enter into the new contract with you, even though the financial condition of our Company was such that we could afford to be very extravagant.[22]

Before receiving the letter, Case, Sponable, and Eldred traveled to the Phonofilm studio to test a new cell. Upon seeing them, de Forest told them he had written off their contract. As Case tersely recalled, "this statement had the effect of greatly shortening our visit."[23] Later de Forest wrote again, saying he was going to use Kuntz cells rather than the Thalofide, an irony considering that it was the Kuntz cells' poor reproduction quality that led him to the Case Lab in the first place. And de Forest's views did not reflect those of his board members. Bolster gave Eldred a copy of the minutes of the December 4, 1925 Phonofilm board meeting, showing that de Forest's views and actions in not accepting the contract proposal had been the minority opinion.[24]

De Forest offered one more proposal, essentially a one-year extension of their previous contract. But by December 8, 1925, the Case-de Forest collaboration was irrevocably over. John Foster Dulles wrote to Case that he thought the situation "ripe for suit."[25] Case and Eldred later wrote to George Compton thanking him for his efforts in the failed negotiations and inviting him to visit the Case Research Lab whenever he was in the Auburn area. But Eldred left no room for misunderstanding. "This is simply an expression of my kind feeling for you and not meant in any way to open up further negotiations—so don't pass it on . . . " he added as a handwritten postscript.[26]

The disintegration of Case and de Forest's collaboration resulted from personality and powerful egos as much as technology and patent issues. The patent situation would always be cloudy. New claims were often built on specific, sometimes subtle equipment alterations, and changes were often based upon general theories developed by earlier inventors. Individual equipment patents were interconnected into the larger sound film systems and arguably open to interpretation by different parties. De Forest, resolutely independent and obstinate about credit and control, preferred to use cheaper products than to acknowledge he was not the primary inventor of his sound film system. He refused to negotiate any point that would adjust the recognition factor in Phonofilm. Case, confident of his system's superiority, proposed outrageous terms he knew de Forest would not accept. Case firmly believed that his sound film system had a profitable commercial future, but de Forest's repeatedly ineffective business management and his inability to master the Case Research Lab's technology were hampering progress. In the end, perhaps even more than concerns over credit, Case wanted to see de Forest removed from the management of Phonofilm. Knowing that situation unlikely, he was willing to go it alone.

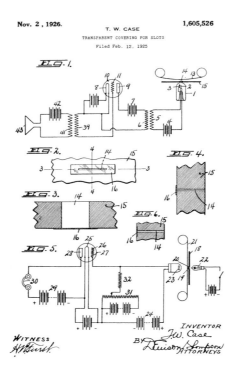

Patent drawing, transparent covering for slots, filed Feb. 12, 1925

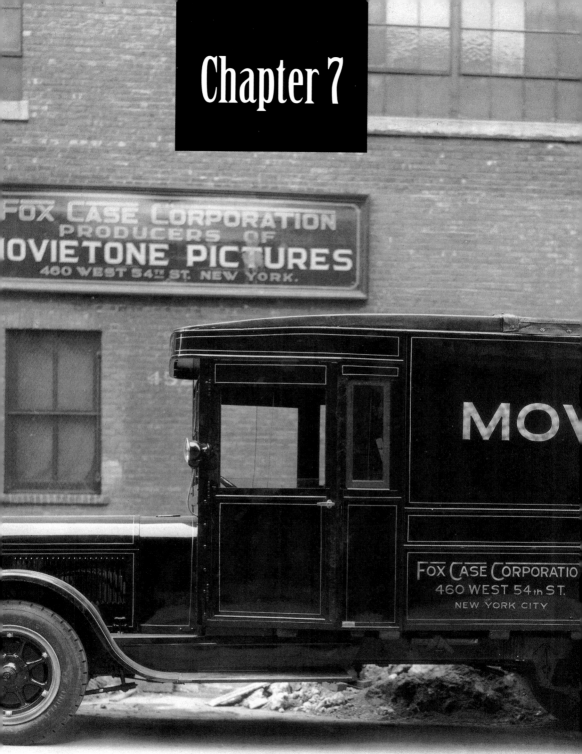

Chapter 7

Fox-Case and Movietone

7

Fox-Case and Movietone

Immediately upon breaking with de Forest, Case and Sponable began visiting major players in the sound film business, trying to negotiate use of amplification equipment and interest other parties in their system. Sponable revisited Western Electric representatives in December 1925, to discuss the possibility of Case using their amplification system for commercial sound films, as they had explored the previous April. But Western Electric's priorities had changed. They were working on their own sound-on-film system, and at the same time negotiating with Warner Brothers, then a secondary film studio open to the possibility of sound pictures, to get a sound-on-disc system to the public.[1]

Edward Craft of Western Electric watched Case's films. He admitted that the Case Research Lab was further along than Western Electric. Craft did not rule out the possibility of collaboration, and sent two Bell Telephone representatives to Auburn to view Case's work. They were likewise impressed, commenting that the simplicity of the Case Research Lab's camera and projector designs could be commercialized easily.[2] Case also tried to interest the manager of the Keith-Albee vaudeville circuit in his talking films. Keith-Albee replied emphatically no. They had been burned twice on the sound film idea, once on Edison's Kinetophone fiasco and later on a de Forest proposition. They did not intend to gamble a third time.

Despite his belief that the lab held a strong position regarding its sound film patents, Case remained concerned over possible litigation by de Forest. During a visit to New York, he and Sponable spoke with Livingston Gifford, a patent attorney who Thompson had highly recommended. Gifford felt Case would prevail in an infringement suit. He later put in writing his belief that the Case Lab could not be attacked successfully under either the de Forest patent for a discharge lamp or the Ries patent (which de Forest had purchased in October 1925) for sound film reproduction.[3]

In early 1926, while the Case Research Lab searched for a partner, Case and de Forest squabbled over the return of Thalofide Cells. Case, Sponable, and Eldred talked extensively with representatives from Bell Telephone, Western Electric, and Radio Corporation of America and hosted visits for their representatives in Auburn. Despite his initial enthusiasm, Craft now told Case that Western Electric could gain little by teaming with him, although he was open to further tests comparing the two systems.[4] Case still held hope for a deal with RCA. But because of cross-licensing agreements between RCA and AT&T (Western Electric's parent company), control of amplification systems was held tightly in Western Electric's grasp. An RCA representative accordingly told Case there was nothing they could do to help. Attempts to interest General Electric also failed.

Having been unable to interest a major player, Case and Sponable turned to previous contacts. In April, Sponable visited Mr. Bassett of Sperry Gyroscope Corporation, who had worked with the lab in the development of the infrared system. Bassett did not know of anyone in a major company, but suggested that Sponable speak with Max Mayer, a theatrical products dealer. Mayer visited Auburn and was impressed with Case's films. But he suggested they needed more appropriate subject matter since singing ducks and other marginal vaudeville acts were not marketable. They also needed to give their system a name. Perhaps Vitaphone, Mayer suggested naively—unaware that the name would soon be preempted by Warner Brothers.[5] Although he did not accept Mayer's advice about a name, Case did consider producing a feature film. He was willing to spend up to $10,000 and allow Mayer to select a cameraman, director, actors, and possible scripts. But the project never reached fruition because the technical limitations of the carriage house studio were not conducive to such a venture.

Theodore Case, Pennington Sefton, Blin Cushman, and Charles Steel, circa 1926.

In April 1926, Warner Brothers and Western Electric formed Vitaphone Corporation to produce sound films, using a sound-on-disc method that synchronized a filmed image with sound recorded on a separate disc. Western Electric granted Vitaphone exclusive license to use its recording and reproducing equipment. By the end of the month, Warner Brothers announced Vitaphone to the press.

Meanwhile, Case, Sponable, and Eldred continued searching for a partner and explored working with Pathé News. Case held little enthusiasm for the prospect but knew that Hayden, Stone & Company would agree to be a financial backer. [6] Case's men tried to interest companies as diverse as Quaker Oats and International Harvester in using talking pictures as an orientation and marketing tool, and Case sent Eldred to pursue the idea of six-foot screens showing talking pictures as advertising billboards in places such as Atlantic City.

A Cornell connection opened the door to more realistic possibilities. In March 1926, John Joy, an old friend of Sponable's from his Cornell days, paid a visit to the Case Research Lab. Joy represented Courtland Smith, who had recently joined Fox Film Corporation and was the secretary of the Motion Picture Producers and Distributors of America. Smith asked Case to come to New York and give a demonstration for his boss, William Fox.

In May, Case formed Zoephone Company, independent of the Case Research Lab, to handle the lab's sound film system. He severed his last ties to de Forest by ending his relationship with British Phonofilms. Case and Sponable demonstrated their sound film system to Fox representatives in New York City at Fox Film's Parlor B on 10th Avenue, and at the Nemo Theater. They also held a private screening at William Fox's home in Woodmere, New York. After overcoming his suspicions, Fox saw possibilities in Case's system and agreed to finance further experiments.[7]

Case's overtures to Fox did not go unnoticed by de Forest, who may have been doubly displeased because he already harbored resentment toward Fox, who a few years earlier had refused to speak to de Forest on a transatlantic crossing.[8] Upon discovering that one of his former employees, Joe Daly, had attended the screening at the Nemo Theater, de Forest grilled him about the proceedings and about Fox's intentions. Daly wrote almost gleefully to Eldred about the heated exchange:

> After wrangling pro and con with both he and his brother he [de Forest] blurted out that he had or was about to serve papers on the Fox Company, as well as William Fox personally, that you were infringing on eight patents and that he was going the limit to prevent you from showing them; also that if I knew of any Exhibitor that was interested in playing same to keep their hands off—that whoever played them was inviting a lawsuit. I told him that this matter was entirely up to him and if I knew of any Exhibitor that was interested in using your product, that I would enthusiastically endorse it. This put him in a rage.[9]

And indeed, de Forest, via his attorney Walter Darby, had sent a letter to Fox Film Corporation warning of infringement on seven patents owned by de Forest:

> We beg to advise you of the fact that our clients, the De Forest Phonofilms, Inc., own and control the basic patents for talking pictures or phonofilms, said patents having been issued to Lee de Forest and Elias Ries, and that the apparatus and films being

exploited by the said Theodore W. Case, or his company
infringes upon these patent rights . . . We know it is not the
desire of your company to become involved in patent litigation
over the above matter, and we therefore trust that in view of the
above facts, you will notify us immediately that you will not
proceed with any further negotiations regarding the use of the
Case apparatus or films.[10]

Fox's representatives were not deterred. Courtland Smith may have had
concerns, but having discussed matters with John Joy and knowing patent
attorney Gifford personally, Smith simply asked Case for a copy of
Gifford's written opinion on the matter. To accompany the report, Eldred
drafted a memo to Fox representatives Courtland Smith and Jack Leo,
briefly outlining reasons to dismiss de Forest's rationale on the five other
patents not listed in Gifford's letter.[11]

Throughout June,
Case and Sponable took
Case Lab recording and
reproducing equipment to
Fox Film Corporation's
building on 10th Avenue
in New York for further
tests and refinement.

Promotional photo, Aeo light, circa 1926.

They made 300,000 feet of test films "to convince Fox of the practicality
of making sound pictures under studio conditions."[12] As Sponable later
recalled, Fox seemed most impressed by a film of a pet canary, which
"chirped and sang at the camera with great realism." The little bird's voice
helped convince the studio magnate to pursue sound-on-film.[13]

On July 23, 1926, Fox-Case Corporation was formed as an independent entity to commercialize the Case Research Lab sound film system.
The new company was owned 25 percent by Fox Films and the remaining
75 percent divided among Fox Theaters, William Fox, and Theodore Case
and his associates. Courtland Smith, who had initially proposed the idea to
Fox, headed Fox-Case Corporation. In the agreement signed by Case and

Fox, Case turned over his patents and commercial rights for the Case Research Lab sound film system to Fox-Case, but the Case Research Lab's permission was required in writing for any changes.[14] For the next three years, the lab would continue to serve as a manufacturing facility for light cells and a developmental facility for Fox-Case. Any resulting patents would belong to that company at its request. Fox-Case Corporation also assumed responsibility for any litigation arising over patents. Fox and Case also agreed that Case would not work solely on the sound film system but use his "reasonable discretion" as to when he was needed by Fox-Case. Case received 2,500 shares of preferred stock and 25,000 shares of common stock. Sponable and Eldred joined the new company in New York to oversee commercializing the system. Case continued to run the Case Research Lab in Auburn.

In August, de Forest filed suit against Fox and Case. The lawsuit was quickly splashed across the pages of the New York press. Almost immediately, de Forest portrayed Case as just an unscrupulous employee:

> Theodore W. Case . . . formerly worked under De Forest at the studio of the latter. It is alleged that at this time he obtained possession of certain trade secrets which he later disposed of to William Fox and which are the basis of the new talking motion picture machine which is being exploited through the Fox theatres. . . . Our relationship was very much that of an employer and an employee.[15]

Although clearly inaccurate, the image was typical of de Forest's tactics. As attorneys postured and litigants jockeyed for position, representatives for both sides stated their arguments over the relative strengths of their cases. An unidentified Fox-Case representative expressed confidence in Case's position relative to the Ries patent:

> In view of the remarkable success of the Case apparatus and its effect upon the court and in view of the fact that nothing was done under the Ries application for so many years after its

filing, and in view of the unsatisfactory demonstrations by the
De Forest Company since acquiring the Ries patent. . . . it is
not believed that any court is likely to permit the Ries patent or
any patent to be granted on the Ries application, to dominate
the Case apparatus.[16]

Earl Sponable in Fox-Case sound studio, New York, circa 1926. Sponable designed
this sound studio, the first purposely created for sound film recording.

Fox-Case moved ahead with plans for its system. Sponable designed
the first professional sound film studios in the United States, built at a
Fox Films annex at 54th Street in New York. "Movietone" became the
trademark for the sound film system. By the end of October, Fox-Case
Corporation held its first tests at the new sound studio.

Case's system was complete except for amplification, requiring Fox-
Case to pursue different avenues for access to amplification rights. In
September, Fox representatives negotiated with General Electric for
commercial use of amplifiers. In October, Case, Sponable, and Eldred
met with representatives of General Electric, Westinghouse, and RCA in
RCA's New York offices to review overall sound film developments. Case
and General Electric made plans to collaborate on tests of their respec-
tive systems.[17]

Fox-Case Movietone truck in front of Movietone studios, New York, circa 1927. This vehicle was a projection truck, used for out-of-doors demonstrations of Movietone newsreels in the United States and Europe.

In the end, negotiations with General Electric fell through. Sponable recalled that the deal was nearly completed, and General Electric had moved equipment to Fox's New York studios. But when signing the papers, William Fox tried to "do a little trimming," in Sponable's words, so General Electric promptly called the deal off and took its equipment back to Schenectady.[18] In later years, this situation would be seen as a big mistake by Fox. He missed an opportunity to dominate sound-film by not pursuing the General Electric agreement. In 1926, the electrical companies' sound film systems—including those of Western Electric and General Electric— were less advanced than Case's system, despite their stranglehold on amplification equipment. With General Electric, Fox-Case could have positioned itself as the leader in the sound film industry.

Vitaphone still held exclusive rights to the amplification equipment, but by November, a sub-licensing agreement with Vitaphone allowed Fox-Case commercial use of Western Electric amplification equipment. By early 1927, Vitaphone and Fox-Case would come to another agreement, ensuring that projection systems in their theaters could be, with minor adjustments, made compatible for playing Vitaphone or Movietone features. These deals

Fox-Case sound film camera, circa 1927.

were the easiest way for Fox to gain access to amplification. In the rush to commercialize sound, they gave him preference for installing sound systems in his theater chain. Unknown to Case, Fox also gave full disclosure of the Case patents to Western Electric. In not pursuing the more independent route, Fox opened the way for access to Fox-Case, and hence the Case Research Lab patents, by companies with less advanced systems. More concerned with expediency, Fox's deals with Western Electric and Vitaphone threw the Fox-Case system into more general use and lessened the value of Case's patents.[19]

Vitaphone premiered to the public on August 6, 1926, with eight sound shorts, including films of banjo player Roy Smeck and noted singer Giovanni Martinelli. The shorts preceded the film *Don Juan*, which featured Vitaphone musical accompaniment. The public reacted enthusiastically, other film studios cautiously. And Vitaphone was not without problems. In December, Eldred wrote Case of a mishap during a Vitaphone showing in New York, which underscored a major drawback of the sound-on-disc system:

> The gossip about town this morning is as follows:
>
> > Last night at the "VITAPHONE"
> > show, when Martinelli came out
> > and opened his mouth to start
> > singing, the audience was
> > greeted with the delightful
> > strains of Roy Smeck's banjo.
>
> It apparently ruined their show, but was amusing to all of us and thought you would like to know about it.[20]

Although wax discs in sound film production seemed logical, and grew out of existing phonograph technology, they proved cumbersome and fallible. They could be difficult to synchronize, easy to mix up, and a single mistake could ruin an evening's entertainment.

Raquel Meller, a Spanish singer featured in one of the first sound shorts produced by Fox-Case, circa 1927.

Unlike de Forest's trumpeting of his system prematurely, Fox-Case acted conservatively (too conservatively in Sponable's opinion), quietly perfecting its sound-on-film system before rushing into the media fray.[21] On January 21, 1927, Fox-Case Movietone made its public debut at the Sam Harris Theater in New York, where unadvertised shorts of Spanish singer Raquel Meller were shown before the silent feature film

What Price Glory. In February, Fox finally hosted a press screening of Movietone. Eldred sent a batch of press clippings glowing with positive comments to Case in Auburn. "The Movietone, guarded these many months by the discrete William Fox and the equally quiet Theodore W. Case, has at last emerged from its quiet nursery . . . into the full glare of limelit success,"[22] proclaimed one source, unwittingly building the image of Case as a reclusive scientist that would become more prevalent in later years.

Lafayette Theater, Batavia, New York, circa 1927. The theater marquee prominently advertised the fact that it could show both Movietone and Vitaphone features.

The first all-Movietone premiere came a few months later, on May 25, 1927 at the Roxy Theater in New York, when Movietone shorts of Chic Sale, Raquel Meller, Ben Bernie's Orchestra, Gertrude Lawrence, and Charles Lindbergh's takeoff from New York to Paris for his transatlantic flight preceded the synchronized-music feature *Seventh Heaven.* The Lindbergh short especially captured audience imagination, alive with the sights and sounds of an instant American hero in the making. It caused the first sensation in sound film.[23] Newsreels like that of Lindbergh's flight underscored the dramatic impact of Movietone on public perception of world events. Sound added dimension to reporting. Famous personalities, including Italian Dictator Benito Mussolini and playwright George Bernard Shaw, appeared before the Movietone cameras. Sporting events

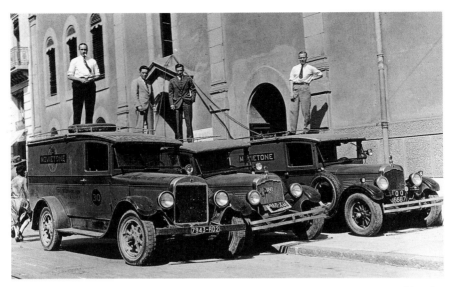

Movietone Newsreel trucks in Europe, circa 1928. Movietone newsreel trucks filmed news events throughout the world.

like the Kentucky Derby proved popular with audiences. Sometimes even gimmicks filmed purely for sound, such as cats fighting and London's Big Ben striking the hour, found their way into Movietone newsreels.

Lee de Forest continued his lonely independent path with De Forest Phonofilm while Warners Brothers Vitaphone and Fox-Case Movietone pioneered sound among the motion picture studios. At one point in 1926, Fox paid $100,000 for an option to buy De Forest Phonofilm, but the transaction was never completed. AT&T representatives told Fox that, because they had already purchased the de Forest radio patents, they owned the rights to the de Forest sound film patents, and de Forest had nothing to sell. This turned out to be wrong, but the confusion underscores the murkiness of the patent situation in the late 1920s.[24] Less than a year later, Fox sued de Forest to get his $100,000 back. De Forest in turn sued several others, claiming that they had made Fox back down on the deal.

De Forest filmed his own version of Lindbergh's transatlantic flight, but it was largely ignored by the major studios. Ironically, in June 1927, the

Roxy and Capitol Theaters in New York featured, respectively, the Fox Movietone and De Forest Phonofilm versions of the event. Case must have felt vindicated by press reaction, but de Forest could not have been pleased:

> A comparison was inevitable, and the Movietone was the victor by the proverbial mile. In fact the contest was so one-sided as to be almost no contest at all. . . . The Phonophilm[sic] offered an interesting depiction of an event of world wide interest— the Movietone a breath-taking transporting of the beholder to the very scenes enacted.[25]

On September 23, the Fox feature *Sunrise*, with Movietone music and effects, premiered, along with shorts of Mussolini. On October 6, the

Warner Brothers motion picture *The Jazz Singer*, with Al Jolson singing and speaking to the audience, caused the first sensation in sound feature films. With Warner Brother's Vitaphone and Fox Movietone leading the way, the battle over sound-on-disc versus sound-on-film had begun, and it signaled the beginning of the end for silent films.

Advertisement for *Sunrise*, 1927.

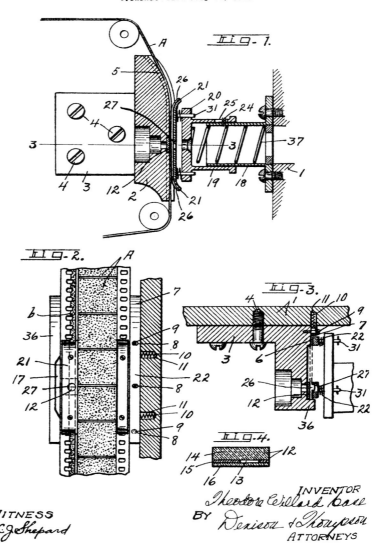

March 20, 1928.

T. W. CASE

TALKING PICTURE MACHINE

Original Filed July 24, 1926

Re. 16,910

WITNESS
L. J. Shepard

INVENTOR
Theodore Willard Case
BY Denison & Thompson
ATTORNEYS

Patent drawing, talking picture machine, filed July 24, 1926.

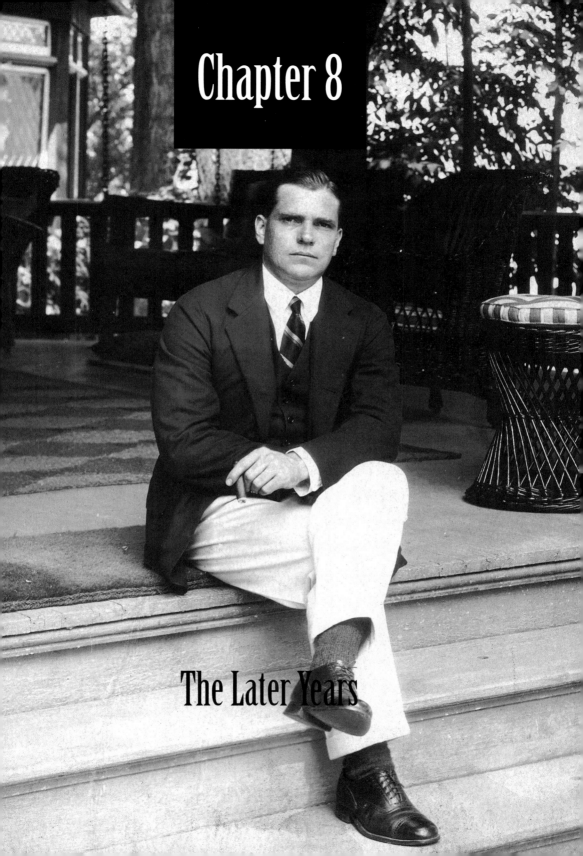

Chapter 8

The Later Years

8

The Later Years

While Fox-Case Movietone pursued commercializing sound film from its New York studios, Theodore Case continued to oversee operations at the Case Research Lab. He traveled periodically between Auburn and New York, conducting studio tests with new light cells and discussing technical ideas or problems with Sponable and the other sound engineers. In July 1928, Case hosted a two-day meeting for Sponable and the Fox-Case engineering team at Casowasco.

Case still played a direct if somewhat vague role in the sound film system developments, but increasingly he came to regard his juxtaposed roles of independent scientist and Fox-Case light cell production manager with unease. From 1928 through 1929, the Case Research Lab functioned mainly as the cell production facility for Fox-Case Corporation, with Case's personnel continuing to refine Aeo lights, manufacture cells, and prepare for defense of the de Forest suit. Case and Sefton, who became Case's main assistant when Sponable departed, spent considerable time training personnel to produce the cells, and they experienced continual problems finding employees with suitable technical skills.

Case was unhappy, because the crunch of daily operations left little time for experimentation. Sandwiched between runs of light cell production, Case would dictate ideas for new inventions. He considered creating a secret signaling system by firing a rapid series of light bursts undetectable to the naked eye due to the persistence of vision. Case proposed a device for removing ice cubes more easily from electric refrigerators using a perforated screen, and he recorded an idea for a device to detect escaping gas in home heating systems.[1]

With patents sold, the base of operations shifted from Auburn to New York. Case seemed to lose interest in sound film, at least as to dealings of the Fox-Case Corporation. He resisted being part of a larger operation where he was not the master of his own fate, a situation that simply did not suit his style. He wanted to reprise his role as a research

Pennington Sefton in Case Research Lab, circa 1927.

scientist and pursue other projects, and he chafed at his inability to do so.

Near the end of 1928, Courtland Smith approached William Fox regarding a new contract with the Case Research Lab that addressed the problem of light cell manufacture. When Case and Fox signed their initial deal, they hoped that a large company such as General Electric or Western Electric would take over actual cell production. The task, however, remained for the Case Research Lab, which manufactured the lights for less than cost while increasing demands for cells pressed the limit of lab facilities and manpower. Fox had been spending up to $55,000 a year on the Case Research Lab, but Smith asked him to increase it to $108,000, including expenses, overhead, and a $2000 a month salary for Case. In the initial agreement, Case had taken no salary, hoping to preserve his independence. But he ended up spending most of his time supervising light cell construction anyway and gradually came to believe that compensation was his due.[2]

Despite the fact that it bore his name, Case began to feel increasingly alienated from Fox-Case Corporation. In notes to a Fox-Case representative before contract negotiations, Case wrote that the original agreement had been drawn so that he was not "under the personal call of Mr. Fox or the corporation which he controlled."[3] In his annual review of lab activities to Fox in 1929, Case pushed for more research time, arguing that Fox films and Movietone would stay ahead of the competition only if they could demonstrate their technical superiority.[4]

But the definition of the competition varied depending on individual interpretations of the players. Staying ahead of the competition simply for the sake of a technically superior system was not foremost in William Fox's mind. He was more concerned with getting the best business advantage for his company and chain of theaters. In the rush to commercialize the Fox-Case Movietone system, the deals Fox made for amplification rights near the end of 1926 and beginning of 1927 allowed Western Electric the right to use all Fox-Case patents. Western Electric, although behind Fox technically, soon perfected a sound-on-film system and, due to its already powerful position with amplification, gained an equipment stronghold. In early 1927, Western Electric formed Electrical Research Products, Inc. (ERPI) as a wholly owned subsidiary to handle sound film business, and Fox-Case ended up being a licensee of ERPI. Because of this agreement, ERPI's sound film system was modeled heavily on Fox-Case's system and based on the patents of the Case Research Lab.[5]

While Fox-Case became entangled in complicated business maneuvers, Lee de Forest became increasingly peripheral in sound film development. He postponed his lawsuit several times following the initial filing in 1926. Sponable and another Fox-Case representative suggested settling with de Forest, mostly over concern that a Fox victory, paradoxically, would throw the gas discharge tube patent into the open. Fox-Case proposed paying de Forest a nominal sum to gain the license to use his patents, plus allowing him to continue granting anyone else the use of his patents as long as Fox-Case received 50 percent of the earnings. In 1928, de Forest sold Phonofilm to a South American and London interest, forming General

Talking Pictures. In 1929, de Forest's suit against Fox-Case was withdrawn, while De Forest Phonofilm of Canada filed another suit against ERPI interests in Canada. When the Canadian suit came to trial in 1931, Case was among those to testify. De Forest lost, the courts deciding that the Case Aeo light did not infringe upon the de Forest patents.[6] In 1933, General Talking Pictures renewed litigation against Fox Film Corporation and Vitaphone regarding the de Forest patents, and in 1935 Lee de Forest finally won a $100,000 judgement.[7]

On February 26, 1929, ERPI agreed to loan William Fox, via Fox Films, $15 million to acquire Loew's Incorporated, the parent company of MGM. In exchange, ERPI was given a general release by William Fox, Fox-Case, and Fox Films of any claims against ERPI, Bell Labs, or Western Electric. The deal might have been good for William Fox, Fox Film Corporation, and Fox Theaters, but the Case Research Lab gained little from it, as it basically gave away the lab's patents. Fox never got the written consent of the Case Research Lab for the transaction, and didn't even inform Case of the agreement.[8] When Case found out what had happened, he didn't record his thoughts, and mentioned nothing in his lab notebooks. But any remaining enthusiasm for the film industry seemed to die. In September 1929, Fox bought the 25 percent interest of Case and his associates in Fox-Case for a total of $1.5 million and stock in the Fox Theaters chain.[9] This deal erased the provisions of the original 1926 agreement between Case and Fox. On January 13, 1930, Fox-Case became Fox Hearst Corporation, and by February 28, Fox-Case Corporation ceased to exist.[10]

With his purchase of Loew's, the ambitious Fox tried to build an empire, but it quickly unraveled around him. Fox had borrowed the $15 million from his competition, and when he was severely overextended, his creditors called the loan in, apparently to end his attempt to dominate the film industry. In early 1930, a group of executives and stockholders, including Harley Clarke of General Theatres Equipment Corporation, ousted William Fox from his company.[11]

Fox Film Corporation's board of directors elected Clarke president in

April 1930, and the studio, which had understandably been in turmoil, began to consolidate operations.[12] In the midst of the confusion, Sponable wrote to Clarke, "I believe I am one of the few that can really be of service to you in connection with the existing . . . problems."[13] Sponable may well have been apprehensive about his future role, because the need for consolidation extended to research and development as well as film production. In 1930, Fox Film Corporation funded research activities at several scattered locations: the Case Research Lab in Auburn, Fox development laboratories in New York and in California, and the laboratory of scientist R. T. Cloud in Chicago.

In 1930, Clarke requested F. R. Moulton visit the Case Lab to assess its future capability as a research and development facility. Moulton, Cloud, Luther Johns (a patent lawyer from Chicago), and Sponable spent three days in Auburn, observing lab activities and assessing the character of its key personnel. Moulton commented that the lab was well equipped and capable of producing the needed cells. But, unlike Case, who believed more research was needed, Moulton felt that the Case Lab was already technologically ahead of current practical applications in the sound film race.

The Case Research Lab faced a crossroads. As Fox expanded, it required greater consolidation of research activities to get the best possible product to theaters as quickly and efficiently as possible. Coordination and control were needed, wrote Moulton, and Fox Films required one person to serve as head of research. Sponable made a strong impression on Moulton. "I am convinced . . . that he [Sponable] is absolutely square and will be whole-heartedly loyal to his organization," Moulton wrote to Clarke. "He obviously is thoroughly familiar with sound development. Moreover, I find that he has the full confidence and respect of Case and the men associated with him. Consequently, so far as the technical aspects of sound are concerned I think he is all that can be desired."[14] The only questions in Moulton's mind were Sponable's quiet demeanor and reticence—not well suited to a leadership role—and his lack of knowledge about color photography, which Moulton thought he could learn quickly.

Moulton's impression of Case? "Mr. Case is a man of considerable

Theodore Case on the steps of the main house at Casowasco, circa 1930.

ability and force. He inherited too much money for the good of his ambition, and since graduation from Yale has not done much except develop sound apparatus in his laboratory. So far as I learned he has no plans for doing anything except work in his laboratory. He is now 42 years of age."[15] Although harsh—and somewhat ironic considering that Case's wealth and independence had enabled him to perfect the sound film system in the first place—the assessment was fairly accurate. Case never needed to work for a living, and had never worked under anyone else. By 1930, he was content to set his schedule on his own time, and he was spending less time in his laboratory.

Case impressed people as a gracious host and man-about-town, (Johns said Case and his wife entertained delightfully at Casowasco during their visit) but he lacked the inner drive more often found in people not born into privileged circumstances. And Case's attitude could be contagious. The previous year, a Fox-Case Movietone newsreel truck had spent time filming in Central New York, stopping in Auburn to consult with Case. The crew was supposed to be recording wild bird songs, but as one of them later recalled, they spent two very pleasant weeks accomplishing nothing before moving on to complete the project in Ithaca.[16]

Johns and Cloud concurred with Moulton's assessment of Case and his lab. Fox could save money, they felt, by transferring research to a central location in a modern, better-furnished laboratory. The Case Research Lab, with its small size and location in an estate backyard in Auburn, was not conducive to expansion into a corporate facility. In fact, Johns felt that the Case Research Lab's entire activities could be consolidated into one room in a general laboratory.

During this visit, Case, unsure about the status of the contract for manufacturing Aeo lights following changes in Fox corporate structure, told the visitors that if the contract was not renewed, he would give up the lab, tear down the Willard mansion, and sell the lot at 203 Genesee Street. He was probably bluffing, perhaps masking his frustration at what he suspected would be the final outcome of the visit.

Case had always been fascinated by science, but he was also a man born to money, from a family deeply imbedded in the Auburn social strata. As young men, Case and Sponable had successfully developed the infrared system and created the sound film system. But the beginning of Sponable's career was the peak of Case's. Sponable, more determined to prove himself professionally and more adaptable to an increasingly corporate structure, made the move to New York, while Case chose not to leave Auburn. He maintained the lab, but his overall focus became fragmented into numerous lesser projects.

With the proceeds from the sale of the patents in 1926, Case built a sprawling neo-gothic style mansion on South Street, the most fashionable neighborhood in Auburn. Designed by a

Enjoying the summer at Casowasco, circa 1930. From left to right: daughter Barbara, mother Eva, Theodore, daughter Jane.

"The Chimneys," under construction, view from the back yard, circa 1930.

"The Chimneys," view from South Street in Auburn.

prestigious Boston architectural firm, "the Chimneys," as the mansion was called, featured a grand ballroom, indoor swimming pool with Egyptian-influenced tile decor, a large staff, and a private studio where Case showed movies to his guests. When not entertaining at the Chimneys, Case held fabulous parties at his summer home, Casowasco (where years ago his father had built his early hydroelectric system). During one memorable Fourth of July circus ball, costumed guests arrived by riding a canvas chute off the upper porch of the house. As they landed on the ground below, they were announced to the assembled guests. The alcohol flowed so freely that, irrespective of class differences, Boston society women and Casowasco staff ended up dancing and partying. Despite his father's long-ago admonishments, Case still favored speedboats and enjoyed fine cigars. He would pilot the steamer *Dorothy* along Owasco Lake's shore, leisurely picking up friends while songs by Bing Crosby and Fred Astaire played on a victrola. Despite the Great Depression, Case's daughter Jane recalled the 1930s as great fun, a time when they were "completely insulated from the rest of the world."[17]

But cultivation of his seemingly charmed world separated Case from his invention. As the sound film business became increasingly commercial-ized and Fox-Case gave way to motion picture industry interests removed from the immediate invention, the field moved on without Case. Sponable, his one-time assistant, was chosen to head Fox's research division.

Theodore Case with camera, 1930s.

Earl and Marie Sponable, with unidentified Movietone representative, during a trip to Brussels, Belgium in 1929. Movietone news crews were in that country filming government officials.

After 1930, the Case Research Lab continued to do some experimental work and produce light cells for Fox Films. While assistants manufactured the cells, Case's ideas tended to wander. He tried to get technicians from Taylor Instrument Company to come to his house to test his idea for a gas detection device. After he had problems with flies sticking to the paint of his mansion, he proposed inventing a house paint with insecticide in it to repel bugs. One afternoon in November 1931, Case called Cushman and Sefton to the Chimneys to witness the results of an experiment he was conducting on an elm tree in his yard. Three months earlier, he had cut some bark away, attached candle wicking parallel to the tree surface, and wrapped it in cotton tape, water-soaked cloth, and asphaltum, trying to prove that the candlewicking would act as a mean of fluid transference and promote the growth of bark.[18]

In early 1932, the Case Research Lab, with Sefton handling the day-to-day activities, was working on an invention of hot filament lights, referred to by Fox people as "hotcat" lights. But changes at Fox signaled the end of the Case Research Lab's role. Because of their agreements with Western Electric and ERPI, in 1932 Fox switched to the Western Electric sound film system for studio work, although it continued to use the Fox-Case system for newsreels. Using someone else's system meant that Fox did not need to conduct its own research, so it eliminated most of its research division. In April, Sponable sent a formal letter to the Case Research Lab, requesting that all experimental and development work on behalf of Fox be discontinued. The lab was to concentrate strictly on manufacturing twenty-four Aeo lights weekly for the newsreel cameras. On the same day, Sponable wrote apologetically to Case, telling him Fox had closed the New York research division. "It is most unfortunate that we could not go through with the work that we are now finishing . . . "[19] Sponable said, referring to the "hotcat" lights. He promised to try and discuss the situation and work things out.

For a few years after 1932, Case continued to dabble in the lab with a small staff, but minus long-time assistant Cushman, who returned to Ithaca in 1933. Sponable visited in March 1933, to discuss patenting the "hotcat" lights, but most direct connections to Fox had faded. When he did spend time in his lab, Case dreamed up whimsical inventions, some with a practical purpose, some without. He came up with an idea of using sound as a by-product of cities, and converting it into electromagnetic energy that could fuel things like neon lights. He made an informal bet with a local man who came to him with a design for a nursing bottle. Case had a design he thought was better; if the other man's idea was patented, he would get the money. If Case's idea was accepted they would split the proceeds fifty-fifty. In 1934, Case recorded a final idea in his lab notes, considering an attempt to photograph the latent image thought to be on the retina of the human or animal eye with infrared rays.

By 1935, the lab was not used, and Case, who had not been serious about tearing down the old Willard mansion, suggested that it and the carriage house be used for a proposed museum in Auburn. Following discussions with artist Walter Long and other community leaders, Case gave the property to the group organizing the museum and loaned the film equipment, with the understanding that the Movietone apparatus would go on display. The Cayuga Museum opened in 1936, and a plaque noting Case's contribution was hung in the hall. The Case Research Lab buildings remained in Case's possession until 1941, when he transferred them to the museum.

Case traveled in Europe and spent time living in an Upper East Side townhouse in Manhattan before he returned to Auburn in the late 1930s. He had lived only a few years in his South Street mansion before handing it over to the city, claiming he couldn't pay the taxes. He seemed a gracious but lost man, and never regained the scientific enthusiasm that had seemed so apparent during the Case Research Lab's heyday. Health problems, including some alcohol-related, became increasingly serious in the late 1930s, and in 1941 Case and his wife Gertrude divorced.

On May 13, 1944, Theodore Case died in Auburn. The official cause of death was listed as pneumonia. The following day, Dwight Eldred cabled Earl Sponable with the news. Among the pallbearers at Case's funeral were Charles Steel, who had been with the lab since the beginning, and John Taber, by then a powerful congressman. Following a funeral at St. Peter's Episcopal Church on Genesee Street, a few blocks from the Case Research Lab, Case was buried in Fort Hill Cemetery in the Willard-Case family plot. The plot, on one of the highest knolls in the cemetery, overlooked the Willard-Case Mansion.

Earl Sponable remained with Fox Film Corporation, becoming a respected authority on the technical development of sound film. In 1927, he created a motion picture screen opaque to images but transparent to sound, allowing loudspeakers to be placed directly behind the screen, heightening the illusion created by sound film.[20] His later projects included Grandeur film and magnetic sound. In 1953, Sponable won an Academy Award for his work on Cinemascope, and he remained Technical Director of the Research and Development Division for Fox, which by that time had become Twentieth Century-Fox Film

Earl Sponable at Twentieth Century-Fox, circa 1953.

Corporation, until his retirement in 1962. In his later years, Sponable always credited Case for the pioneering sound film work they had done in the 1920s. Sponable spent his final years with his wife Marie and daughter Catherine in Lake Placid, New York, where he died in 1977.

The Case Research Lab's brief period of operation coincided with a time of rapid technological change, and Case's wealth allowed him and his associates the freedom to operate outside the confines of a university or commercial motion picture studio setting. Case was fortunate to have quality people, especially Earl Sponable, working with him. Even his collaboration with de Forest, contentious as it was, proved fortuitous, and it provided the catalyst that led to Fox-Case Movietone. Although today neither Theodore Case or the Case Research Lab are household names, their legacy lives on in the enjoyment that sound film has brought to generations of motion picture audiences.

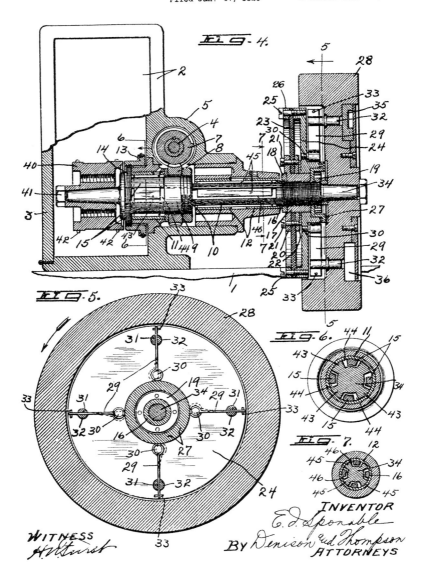

Aug. 30, 1932.   E. I. SPONABLE   1,874,712

COMBINED MOVING PICTURE AND SOUND CAMERA

Filed Jan. 17, 1929   3 Sheets—Sheet 2

Patent drawing, Earl Sponable, combined motion picture and sound camera, filed Jan. 17, 1929

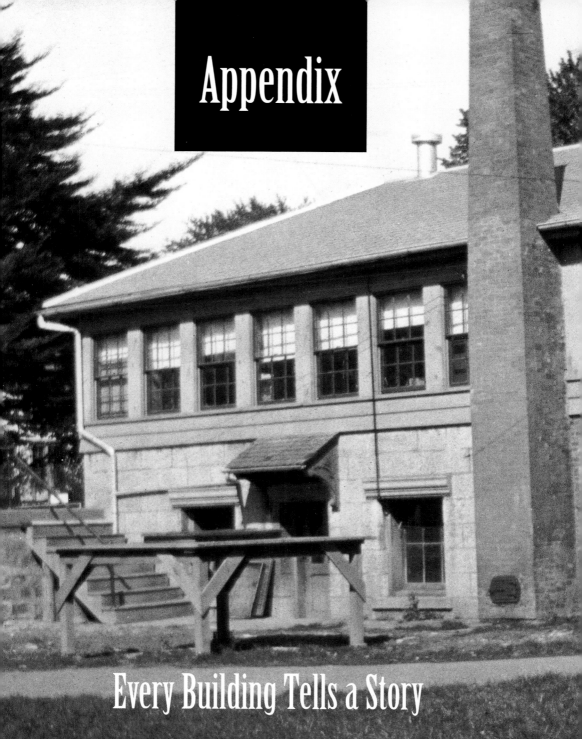

Appendix

Every Building Tells a Story

by Jim Richerson

Every Building Tells a Story

by Jim Richerson

A primary resource for the history of the Case Research Lab (CRL) is the building, its relationship to surrounding structures, and various documents that reflect changes in its use through the succeeding years. The lab developed on the masonry foundation of a former greenhouse on the Willard/Case estate. Still evident in the remaining CRL building are some of Case's changes to his lab. Documents in the collection of the Cayuga Museum tell of the struggle to guard the building and its contents. Now, more than sixty years later, the museum operates with a clearer sense of mission, which includes long-range preservation and interpretative planning of this important history. In deference to past Cayuga Museum directors, it must be noted that considerably more assistance and expertise is now available to help museums research and fund such projects.

Resources used in the preparation of this appendix include tax and survey maps, evidence from the building and surrounding grounds, references in the lab's notebooks, correspondence, photographs, annual reports, museum directors' files and board meeting minutes, all available in the Cayuga Museum archives.

Events Shaping the Case Research Lab (CRL):

In 1916, Willard E. Case inherited the 203 Genesee Street property from the estate of his cousin Caroline Willard. Theodore W. Case and his father, Willard E. Case, immediately converted one of the estate's three greenhouses into a laboratory. They called it the Case Research Lab.

In 1918, the lab expanded, absorbing a smaller wooden structure some twenty feet to the south. Willard Case died in the Spanish Influenza epidemic that year.

By late 1924, Case had expanded his operation to include the carriage house. He turned the second floor into a sound test studio. Here he filmed a variety of local and out-of-town performers, including vaudeville acts. Originally, the sound studio had been located in the north basement of the CRL. By 1926, Case had fashioned a theater out of the first floor of the carriage house.

During 1927, Case converted the upper floors of the mansion into the Logan school. The school taught elementary age children of wealthy families, including the Case children.

By 1931, Case moved his family to their new 108 South Street mansion. He used the 203 Genesee Street mansion as an office on the first floor. The lower level supported the production work in the lab.

During 1934, a group of citizens including Walter K. Long, then an instructor at the College of Arts in Syracuse, began searching for a location in Auburn for a Civic Arts Center. In 1935, Case approached the group offering them his 203 Genesee Street mansion as an art center and to house an exhibit featuring his sound film invention. In June 1936, the Cayuga Museum of History and Art was created in the Willard/Case mansion and carriage house, which Case referred to as a barn. On December 7, Case drew up an agreement loaning his "Movietone" apparatus, other related equipment and films to the museum for public exhibition. Case maintained control of the CRL and a smaller concrete block house to the west, where he stored test films. In 1941, Case deeded the lab to the museum for an exhibition centered around his system of sound on film. The concrete block house was also included in the deed. That year, with Case's help, the City of Auburn deeded to the museum a vacant property located immediately west of the Willard/Case estate. Also that year, a community theater group worked out an agreement with the museum for long-term use of the carriage house for productions.

Until Case's death in 1944, Walter K. Long (Cayuga Museum director from 1936-1986) had numerous conversations with Case about creating a permanent exhibition documenting Case's sound film invention.

By 1947, E.I. Sponable and Long approached Fox to fund the restoration of the CRL as a permanent public exhibition. (Sponable had been an assistant of Case's from 1916-1926, but by then was Technical Director of Research and Development for Twentieth Century-Fox.) Through 1948, records indicate various strategies pursued for funding an exhibition on Case's work to be located in the lab building. Anticipated funding for the Case exhibition from Twentieth Century-Fox was finally shelved because of a general loss in revenues due to a film embargo imposed on American films to foreign countries.

In 1949, the museum converted space in the lab for children's art classes. The concrete block house was also rearranged for use as general storage. By 1950, a general reorganization of the lab building created an art studio for adult and children's art education programs sponsored by the museum. In the early 1950s museum records note that much of Case's equipment was oiled and packed for storage. In 1952, a fire in the concrete block house destroyed many of Case's test films pertinent to sound film development.

During 1961, the twenty-fifth anniversary of the museum's founding, Long tried to procure city and county funding for a permanent exhibition documenting Case's work. This effort bore no fruit.

On September 13, 1973, the Willard/Case mansion suffered a devastating fire in the attic started by a workman's torch. The original sound film camera was destroyed in the fire. Plans to restore what was left of the camera were never pursued, and the remnants were lost.

In 1976, the creation of the Schweinfurth Memorial Art Center made it necessary to obtain a portion of land to the west of the museum. Museum officials notified Case's heirs of these intentions. The Art Center and the Cayuga Museum were set up as separate institutions.

On February 24, 1977, Case's heirs signed an agreement relinquishing all claims to Case's equipment and allowing for a portion of land to be given over for the creation of an art center. To appease Case's heirs, the museum created a fund of $15,000 for the purpose of a permanent sound film exhibition in the Willard/Case mansion. The north parlor on the first floor was designated for the exhibit. In late spring 1977, the Case exhibition opened in the Willard/Case mansion. Letters on file from Barbara (Case) Kissel and Theodore (Bill) W. Case, Jr. expressed their delight and appreciation to Long for the exhibit's content and presentation.

In 1980, the Schweinfurth Memorial Art Center opened. With its opening, arts activities previously held in the lab and carriage house were made redundant. During the 1980s the various clubs and drama activities in the lab and carriage house faded away, and the buildings became storage units. The lab and carriage house began to suffer from deferred maintenance.

In November 1986, the Cayuga Museum executive director, Marion Balyzak, contacted film technicians at the George Eastman House in Rochester, N.Y., about preserving the remaining nitrate experimental films produced by Case. Approximately 3,000 feet of film, containing significant sound-on-film accomplishments, was transferred to video tape.

In 1990 executive director Peter L. Jones renewed interest in the CRL and its collections. In 1991, Jones secured funds to copy a complete set of the lab's notebooks and began to research the CRL's history. In 1993, with $65,000 awarded in matching funds from the New York State Environmental Protection Fund, the CRL building was restored. Additional funding was secured from Cayuga Savings Bank and a local foundation. The services of Crawford and Stearns, a Syracuse, NY based architectural firm specializing in historic preservation, were engaged for this restoration project.

In March 1994, the museum hired a professionally trained curator, Stephanie Przybylek, who was charged with gathering the Case collection that was dispersed throughout museum buildings. In June 1994, the Case Research Lab Museum was dedicated and opened to the public containing an initial interpretive exhibit. In 1995, the museum received a New York State Council on the Arts (NYSCA) grant to develop a collection management plan for the Case collection. In 1996, with $44,000 awarded in matching funds from the New York State Environmental Protection Fund, exterior work on the carriage house, where Case's sound studio was located, commenced. During 1996, the museum received a NYSCA grant to systematically inventory, research and catalog the Case collection. In 1997, the museum received a NYSCA grant to publish its research, resulting in the creation of this book.

In 1998, a new standing-seam metal roof and major masonry restoration were completed for the carriage house. A plan to renovate the interior has also been scheduled after some pressing needs for the museum's main building, the Willard/Case mansion, are addressed.

Observations made in the late 1990s compared with earlier Photographic and Survey Records:

The Willards prided themselves on the extensive gardens of their 203 Genesee Street urban estate. In Dr. Sylvester Willard's house ledger he recorded numerous expenditures for gardening supplies. A late nineteenth-century photo taken from the second floor north-facing window of the mansion shows three greenhouse buildings (fig. 1). Upon inheriting the estate in 1916, T. W. Case and his father, Willard Case, refashioned the greenhouse nearest the carriage house to suit their scientific pursuits and created the CRL on this site.

During the Cases' first year of occupancy, they completely rebuilt the small one-story greenhouse located just southeast of the carriage house.

(fig. 1) **Willard-Case estate, view of greenhouses and carriage house, late 19th century. This photograph was taken from a second story window of the mansion.**

Upon an existing foundation, the Cases constructed a frame building with a traditional truss roof and ample windows on all four sides. A photograph from 1916 (fig. 2) shows a building approximately half the length of the CRL that exists today. The view of the structure from the west shows the old foundation, but with a new structure sporting multiple-paned windows, new roof complete with metal venting and chimney standing more than two stories. The chimney was built in conjunction with a glass-blowing workshop in the basement to produce glass tubes. The floor was made of concrete vaults spanning iron I-beams. A wood floor was not used because of the fire hazards from the glass-blowing furnace below. In a 1916-1917 photograph, immediately to the south is a separate clapboard building. It was demolished when the lab was extended during the spring of 1918, as noted in the lab journal.

Internal investigations of the current structure show two separate basement sections. The CRL's southern addition absorbed another structure of unknown use. A stone and earth-filled wall of approximately fourteen feet still separates the basement sections with only a crawl space connecting them, allowing for heating, water and electrical pipes. CRL notes and physical evidence indicates that a machine shop was

(fig. 2) **Case Research Lab, circa 1916. This view shows a wood frame building to the right of the original lab structure that was removed to make way for lab expansion in 1918.**

(fig. 3) **Case Research Lab, late 1980s.** This view shows the lab structure as it was after the 1918 addition. Three different types of stonework are visible in the foundation. This image also shows the condition of the building prior to restoration. Note the causeway which connected the lab building to the carriage house.

in the southern section. Several of the pulleys, related brackets and motors remain. At the southern and northern extremes of the building massive pipes exit the structure. These pipes, which run to the mansion, indicate a central heating system for the entire estate with the boiler in the basement of the carriage house. It has not been determined when this central heating system was installed or went out of use.

On the upper story, lab notes and physical evidence indicate the changing of darkroom locations from the northern portion of the building to the southern end. The floor changes from concrete in the northern section to wood in the southern, newer section. This expansion coincided with accelerated CRL activities during WWI when Case was devising an infrared signaling system for the U.S. Navy, as well as producing more tubes for his experiments with light and electricity. A photograph of the west view of the lab from the early 1980s shows three sections of foundation (fig. 3). Sadly, the photo also shows the degradation of the building. The southwestern foundation corner has fallen away, roof shingles are missing and all windows are boarded up. The photo reveals a causeway that was built by the museum in the 1950s connecting

(fig. 4) **View of carriage house and block house, prior to demolition of block house for construction of Schweinfurth Art Center in 1980. This location is now a parking lot.**

the lab and carriage house. This causeway was removed in the early 1990s just before the CRL's renovation.

A February 1980 photograph shows the concrete block house situated just south of the carriage house level with the basement of the CRL (fig. 4). This building was razed shortly after the photo was taken to make room for a parking lot behind the Schweinfurth Memorial Art Center.

A mid-1990s photo, after restoration, shows the building much the way it appeared in the 1920s, when the lab was operating at full capacity (fig. 5).

The Case Research Lab Museum now operates as part of the Cayuga Museum. Staff lead visitors through the lab where they can view Case's office, the darkroom and a chemistry room. A large workroom on the north side, which occupies the original 1916 lab area, contains exhibits and explanatory text about Case's activities including infrared and sound film systems (fig. 6). With a better understanding of Case's work through research and the publication of the CRL's history, the museum envisions an in-depth and interactive exhibition. Plans call to restore the carriage house theater. This space will be used as a general museum orientation space,

(fig. 5) **Case Research Lab, western view after restoration, 1994.**

including a video presentation about Theodore W. Case and the invention of sound on film. Case's sound stage, located on the second floor of the carriage house, is also part of the planned restoration and presentation.

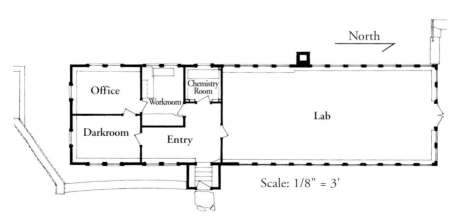

(fig. 6) **Case Research Lab, ground plan done in early 1990s, prior to restoration, showing room configuration after 1918 additions. Image courtesy Crawford and Stearns, Architects and Preservation Planners.**

Footnotes

Unless otherwise noted all correspondence, notebooks, newspaper articles and other archival sources are housed in the Case Research Lab collection at the Cayuga Museum.

Introduction

1   Correspondence, Lee de Forest to Walter Long, March 13, 1958.

Chapter 1

1   Correspondence, Jacob Gould Schurman to Willard Case, May 8, 1908; May 23, 1908; and May 28, 1908. Letters bound in letter books, Volumes 1-80. Jacob Gould Schurman Papers, Department of Manuscripts, Cornell University Library, Ithaca, New York.

2   Correspondence, Frederick I. Allen to Willard Case, May 20, 1908.

3   Written on margin of a letter, Willard Case to Theodore Case, 1910. Original in the collection of Theodore W. Case Jr.

4   Correspondence, T. W. Case to Eva Caldwell Case, January 22, 1911.

5   Correspondence, T. W. Case to Eva Caldwell Case, February 12, 1911.

6   This investment would not provide a return until the film inventions were patented in 1926. Anthony Cardinale, "The Sound of Light," *Buffalo Magazine*, January 19, 1992, p. 9.

7   Recollection of Catherine "Mimo" Sponable, Earl Sponable's daughter. Phone conversation with Marie Eckhardt, October 1, 1977.

8   Correspondence, Willard Case to T. W. Case, undated letter filed in 1916 records.

9   Ibid.

10   Correspondence, Willard Case to George Guy, September 2, 1916.

Chapter 2

1   Case's statement quoted by Marguerite Mooers Marshall, "Electricity Free as Water, Air or Light When Young Mr. Case Harnesses the Sun," *The Evening World*, June 1916. Article pasted in Case scrapbook I.

2   Ibid.

3   Correspondence, De Forest Radio Telephone & Telegraph Co. to Case Research Lab, April 11, 1917.

4   CRL Notebook 1, Sept. 1, 1917, p. 6. Sponable wrote "Reported to W. E. Case by phone. He advised dropping work…as our method did not appear satisfactory…."

5   CRL Notebook 1, July 25, 1917, pp. 60, 82-88.

6   CRL Notebook 2, April 10-14, 1918, p. 55.

7   CRL Notebook 2, May 3, 1918, p. 68.

8   Correspondence, U. S. Patent Office to Theodore Case, July 15, 1918.

9   CRL Notebook 3, April 20, 1918, p. 59.

10 Correspondence, T. T. Beloire, Curator, Division of History, to W. de C. Ravenel, June 2, 1919; W. de C. Ravenel to G. Winchester, June 4, 1919; Earl Sponable to Smithsonian Institution, June 9, 1919. Accession 63751. All material from accession files of Electricity Collection, National Museum of American History, Smithsonian Institution. Other materials may still exit in the Military Collection at the Smithsonian.

Chapter 3

1   CRL Notebook 6, April 24, 1920, p. 30.

2   CRL Notebook 9, Feb. 2, 1922, p. 12.

3   "Mr. Case suggested that the fact that the human eye is sensitive to the green might be explained according to the theory of evolution in that man might have at one time been a fish. If such were the case the eye of the fish would have received mainly green light in as much as most bodies of water transmit the green when viewed beneath the surface of the water." CRL Notebook 8, March 9, 1921, p. 1.

4   CRL Notebook 6, March 26, 1920, p. 17.

5   CRL Notebook 6, August 19, 1920, p. 71.

6   Recollections of Mimo Sponable, phone conversation with Marie Eckhardt, October 1, 1997; correspondence, Stephanie Przybylek to Mimo Sponable, February 22, 1999. Earl Sponable and Marie B. Whalen graduated from Auburn Evening School in 1917, and were married on September 7, 1918.

7   Theodore and Gertrude had two other children in the years that followed—Jane in 1923 and John in 1926.

8   Correspondence, Lee de Forest to Case Research Lab, August 26, 1920.

9   Correspondence, Theodore Case to Lee de Forest, September 3, 1920.

10 Correspondence, Lee de Forest to Case Research Lab, November 10, 1920.

11 CRL Notebook 8, March 22, 1921, p. 2.

12 CRL Notebook 7, December 10-16, 1920, p. 22.

13 CRL Notebook 8, April 22,1921, p. 8. "Chemist Will Measure Light of New Lamps," *Syracuse Post-Standard*; "Mr. Case to Aid City in Street Light Quandry," *Auburn Advertiser-Journal*; both newspaper articles pasted in Case's scrapbook between December 1920 and Oct. 1921.

14 CRL Notebook 9, "Infra-Red Telegraphy and Telephony," April 1922, p. 50.

Chapter 4

1   "The Life and Work of Lee De Forest," Part II, *Radio News*, November 1924, pp. 658, 1091. This nine part serialized article ran in the years when de Forest was a household name. A copy of the article was found among the documents in the Case Research Lab files. The article attributed some of de Forest's less generous personality traits to his solitary upbringing. De Forest's life and career in radio, as well as his sound-on-film work, is discussed at considerable length in Tom Lewis, *Empire of the Air: The Men Who Made Radio* (New York: Harper Collins, 1991). De Forest is also the subject of a full-length biography, which is strongly weighted in his favor. Georgette Carneal, *Conqueror of Space: The Life of Lee De Forest* (New York: Horace Liveright, 1930). Note: the spelling of de Forest's name reflects his preferred use of the lowercase "d" when signing correspondence. When referring to the company, his name always appeared as De Forest Phonofilm Corporation.

2   The high frequency discharge tube, also called a gas glow tube, would later become a point of dispute between Case and de Forest. De Forest did create a crudely working tube that he called a photion light, but he was dissatisfied with the results and dropped the idea. CRL Notebook 10, December 15, 1922, p. 26. De Forest's experience in Germany was not positive. He had continual problems with finances and personnel. Lewis, *Empire of the Air*, p. 171.

3   Unidentified newspaper article, April 23, 1922. Article pasted in Case scrapbook.

4   E. E. Ries visited the Case Research lab in 1923 and tried to sell his patents to Case. Tykociner visited the Case Research Lab in 1927 and signed an agreement with Case for an option to purchase his invention for $2000 but the transaction was never completed. The document remains in the Case Research Lab collection.

5   De Forest later recalled his first tests, around November 1922, "I well remember the grim satisfaction I felt when, for the first time in reproducing a photographic record of my voice, I was able to clearly determine whether or not it was being run backwards!" Sponable, "Historical Developments of Sound Film," *SMPE Journal* 48: 4-5, April and May 1947, p. 286.

6   Correspondence, Case Research Lab to Lee de Forest, September 18, 1922.

7   Correspondence, T. W. Case to Lee de Forest, September 18, 1924; Lee de Forest to T. W. Case, September 22, 1922; T. W. Case to Lee de Forest, September 26, 1924; Lee de Forest to T.W. Case, September 28, 1922.

8   "During this time, Case saw Rankine's sound record in London with Dr. Sefton (Ruhmer's type of record) This interested Case in pursuing the subject on his return." Unpublished manuscript, Case Chronology, Memorandum Aug. 20, 1929. This document was written by Case during the years involving litigation with de Forest.

9   Correspondence, Lee de Forest to Theodore Case, undated letter filed with November 1922 records.

10   CRL Notebook 10, Nov. 27, 1922, p. 25.

11   Correspondence, Case Research Lab to Lee de Forest, November 29, 1998.

12   Deposition draft, CRL Notebook 10, December 14, 1922, between pp. 27-28.

13   Ibid.

14   Aeo stands for alkaline earth oxides, the composition of elements used to coat the platinum cathode in the light.

15   Deposition draft, CRL Notebook 10, December 14, 1922, between pp. 27-28.

16   Correspondence, John Taber to Lee de Forest, December 16, 1922.

17   Correspondence, Lee de Forest to John Taber, December 18, 1922.

18   Ibid.

19   CRL Notebook 10, Dec. 15, 1922, p. 26; March 18, 1923, Statement by T. W. Case on his work in connection with the "Talking Movie" work by Lee De Forest. "I did not become further interested experimentally in Dr. De Forest's project until he sent me some of his photion lights . . . "

20   CRL Notebook 10, December 22, 1922, p. 29.

21   Correspondence, Lee de Forest to Case Research Lab, December 31, 1922.

22   CRL Notebook 10, January 9, 1923, pp. 32-35. De Forest filmed his shorts at the Tec-Art Studio on 318 East 48th Street, New York City.

23   CRL Notebook 10, January 16, 1923, p. 37.

24   CRL Notebook 10, February 23-24, 1923, p. 45.

25   Ibid.

26   CRL Notebook 10, March 13, 1923, pp. 47-48.

27   CRL Notebook 10, March 13, 1923. pp. 48, 50.

28   Correspondence, John Taber to Lee de Forest, March 15, 1923.

29   Correspondence, Lee de Forest to T. W. Case, March 17, 1923.

30   Correspondence, Lee de Forest to T. W. Case, March 17, 1923.

31   "I do not go into details as regards the latter, because it would be most unwise at this time to disclose to Outsiders just what is being employed in the camera." Correspondence, Lee de Forest to T. W. Case, March 17, 1923.

32   "Notable 'Pictures That Talk' Invention by Local Scientist," *Auburn Advertiser-Journal*, March 17, 1923. Article pasted in Case scrapbook.

33   "Talking Movies Invented by Auburn Man Through Aid of Strong Light Ray," *Syracuse Herald*, March 18, 1923; and "Think Speaking Film is At Hand," *New York Herald*, March 18, 1923. Articles pasted in Case scrapbook.

34   Correspondence, T. W. Case to Lee de Forest, March 25, 1923.

35   E. Donaldson Clapp was the treasurer of E. D. Clapp Company, a successful drop forge and coal dealer in Auburn.

36   Correspondence, Lee de Forest to T. W. Case, March 31, 1923.

37   Correspondence, E. Donaldson Clapp to T. W. Case, April 5, 1923.

Chapter 5

1   *New York Times*, April 16, 1923. Article pasted in Case scrapbook. Several of de Forest's Phonofilms exist in the Zouary Collection in the Library of Congress. But, according to former Cayuga Museum director Peter Jones, researchers should note that the films are mislabeled as to production dates space (the listed dates are a few years earlier than they should be).

2   Correspondence, Edwin Hopkins to T. W. Case, July 4, 1923. Hopkins was another inventor interested in sound film.

3   Correspondence, Lee de Forest to T. W. Case, April 17, 1923. "I am anxious, also, to make some arrangement with you whereby Mr. Sponable can spend, say, three days each week in the studio while we are making records to look after the amplifying and sound photography problems during my absence."

4   CRL Notebook 11, May 13-14, 1923, p. 13.

5   Correspondence, Lee de Forest to T. W. Case, May 27, 1923.

6   Correspondence, W. E. Waddell to T. W. Case, May 28, 1923.

7   Correspondence, T. W. Case to Lee de Forest, May 29, 1923.

8   CRL Notebook 11, including entries for June 28, 1923, p. 27; August 31-September 5, 1923, pp. 35-36; September 17, 1923, p. 39.

9   "The Gas-Filled Lamp That Photographs Sound," *The World*, May 27, 1923; de Forest, "When Light Speaks," *Scientific American*, August 1923; Fred E. Baer, "Giving the Film a Voice," *The Evening World Radio*, August 11, 1923; "Talking Movies Again Demonstrated by Case," *Auburn Citizen*, September 15, 1923. Articles pasted into Case scrapbook.

10   Correspondence, William O. Dapping to T. W. Case, September 14, 1923.

11   CRL Notebook 11, December 11, 1923, p. 63.

12   Correspondence, Lee de Forest to T. W. Case, November 3, 1923. De Forest contended that Gaumont had double-crossed him on an earlier deal. Case sent a single cell to Gaumont Studios on behalf of W. R. Whitney of General Electric Co. in July 1923. Correspondence, Case Research Lab to L. Gaumont, Société des Etablissments Gaumont, July 28-Sept. 14, 1923. Gaumont had requested that Whitney contact the Case Research Lab, because he knew de Forest was using Case's photoelectric cells in his recordings. Correspondence, W. R. Whitney, General Electric Co., to T. W. Case, July 20, 1923.

13   Correspondence, Lee de Forest to T. W. Case, November 14, 1923.

14   Correspondence, Lee de Forest to T. W. Case, December 31, 1923; T. W. Case to Lee de Forest, December 31, 1923.

15   CRL Notebook 11, January 2, 1924, p. 66. The recording was of Dr. Frank Crane.

16   CRL Notebook 11, January 15, 1924, p. 73.

17   CRL Notebook 11, January 18-23, 1924, p. 73.

18   CRL Notebook 11, January 18, 1923-February 6, 1924, pp. 73-77.

19   Correspondence, E. I. Sponable to T. W. Case, February 25, 1924.

20   Robert E. Sherwood, "Motion Pictures Column," *New York Herald*, Monday February 11, 1924. Article pasted into Case scrapbook.

Footnotes

21   Correspondence, Lee de Forest to T. W. Case, February 11, 1924.

22   Correspondence, Hugo Riesenfeld to W. E. Waddell, De Forest Phonofilm, February 13, 1924; W. E. Waddell to T. W. Case, February 27, 1924; Lee de Forest to T. W. Case, February 28, 1924. Riesenfeld and de Forest had strong mutual ties. Riesenfeld had helped finance De Forest Phonofilm Corporation. He was also a composer as well as theater director, and de Forest had recorded Riesenfeld's score for *The Covered Wagon* in 1924.

23   "Talking Motion Pictures," *Auburn Advertiser-Journal*, June 5, 1924, p. 4; "Talking Movies Invented by Case Stir Wonder," *Auburn Advertiser-Journal*, June 9, 1924, p. 6; "Co-inventor of Talking Movies Visits Auburn," *Auburn Advertiser-Journal*, June 28, 1924, p. 7.

24   Correspondence, Lee de Forest to T. W. Case, July 2, 1924.

25   Correspondence, D. B. Eldred to Lee de Forest, July 9, 1924; Lee de Forest to T. W. Case, July 17, 1924; W. E. Waddell to T. W. Case, July 22, 1924.

26   Correspondence, Lee de Forest to T. W. Case, July 7, 1924.

27   *Auburn Advertiser-Journal*, July 18, 1924, p. 7. Landis, a Chicago native and avid baseball fan, became the first Commissioner of Baseball following his successful prosecution of several Chicago White Socks players who tried to throw the World Series in 1919 (also known as the infamous Chicago "Black Socks" scandal). Landis came through Auburn to visit John H. Farrell, then Secretary of the National Association of Professional Baseball Clubs. Correspondence, D. B. Eldred to Lee de Forest, August 4, 1924.

28   Correspondence, Lee de Forest to T. W. Case, July 25, 1924. "I suppose you will have your camera ready on a day's notice, and inasmuch as you have your amplifier already adapted for the carbon microphone, would it not be better for you to bring the apparatus to Washington and put it on a truck . . . and then drive the whole thing up to the White House? E. I. could go along and we would supply our good camera man, Blakely."

29   CRL Notebook 12, August 11, 1924, p. 14. Case and Sponable recorded notes during this trip, and both versions are included in the Case Lab notebooks.

30   CRL Notebook 12, August 11, 1924, p. 8.

31   CRL Notebook 12, August 11, 1924, p. 14. In fairness to Coolidge, his demeanor must also have reflected a recent personal tragedy. His son Calvin Coolidge Jr. died on July 8, just a few weeks before Phonofilm production.

32   CRL Notebook 12, August 11, 1924, p. 15.

33   CRL Notebook 12, August 11, 1924, p. 15.

34   Ibid.

35   CRL Notebook 12, August 11, 1924, p. 9.

36   CRL Notebook 12, August 11, 1924, p. 15.

37   CRL Notebook 12, August 11, 1924, p. 16. Case recorded that these films were taken with strontium Aeo light 938.

38   Correspondence, T. W. Case to J. H. McNabb, Bell & Howell, Sept. 4, 1924; J. H. McNabb, Bell & Howell to T. W. Case, Sept. 9, 1924.

39   Correspondence, D. B. Eldred to Lee de Forest, August 28, 1924.

40   Correspondence, D. B. Eldred to Lee de Forest, August 28, 1924.

41   Correspondence, Lee de Forest to T. W. Case, August 28, 1924.

42   Correspondence, T. W. Case to Lee de Forest, September 16, 1924.

43   Correspondence, Lee de Forest to T. W. Case, September 26, 1924; T. W. Case to Lee de Forest, September 19, 1924.

44   Correspondence, D. B. Eldred to Lee de Forest, October 9, 1924.

45   Correspondence, T. W. Case to W. E. Waddell, De Forest Phonofilm, October 16, 1924.

46   Correspondence, W. E. Waddell, De Forest Phonofilm, to T. W. Case, October 18, 1924.

47   Correspondence, Lee de Forest to T. W. Case, November 12, 1924; Lee de Forest to T. W. Case, November 14, 1924.

48   Correspondence, T. W. Case to Lee de Forest, October 29, 1924; T. W. Case to Lee de Forest, November 15, 1924.

49   Correspondence, W. E. Waddell, De Forest Phonofilm, to T. W. Case, November 29, 1924. The debate continued through November, and finally ended with a terse cable from Case on December 3, 1924, "Am not sending Sponable or print to New York."

50   E. I. Sponable, "Historical Development of Sound Film," *SMPE Journal* 48: 4-5, April and May 1947, p. 296. Craft was head of the Engineering Department at Western Electric. He became Vice President of Bell Laboratories when it was formed by a merging AT&T and Western Electric's Research Departments in 1925.

Chapter 6

1   Correspondence, Case Research Lab to Gertrude Vayo, Eastman School of Music, May 18, 1925.

2   Correspondence, Lee de Forest to T. W. Case, March 5, 1925.

3   *Phonofilm Sales Booklet*, mounted in CRL Notebook 12, p. 56.

4   Correspondence, T. W. Case to R. K. Squire, *New York World*, May 18, 1925.

5   Correspondence, T. W. Case to C. F. Elwell, April 27, 1925.

6   Correspondence, T. W. Case to Lee de Forest, May 23, 1925.

7   Correspondence, T. W. Case to E. I. Sponable, May 4, 1925.

8   Correspondence, E. I. Sponable to T. W. Case, May 11, 1925.

9   The story of the reckless stock selling scheme was splashed across the NYC papers for several weeks. "Elliot Back, Ballyhooing Stocks with Coolidge Bait," *New York Herald & Tribune*, May 6, 1925; "Coolidge Film Used as 'Bait,'" *New York American*, May 7, 1925; "Elliot Film Bait Vexing to Coolidge," *New York Herald & Tribune*, May 7, 1925; "Federal Scrutiny of Elliot Sales," *New York World*, May 7, 1925; and "State Seizes Elliot Film Sales Book," *New York Herald & Tribune*, May 8, 1925. Case assiduously collected the clippings press services sent him and pasted them into his scrapbook.

10   Marjorie Waters called the Case Research Lab one of the greatest achievements in Auburn's history. She perhaps overstated the lab's importance, but her statement reflected Case's high recognition in Auburn in the 1920s. Marjorie Waters, "Auburn to Show Her Wares," *Finger Lakes Topics*, June 6, 1925. Pp. 4, 20.

11   Correspondence, C. H. Elwell, De Forest Phonofilms Ltd., to T. W. Case, June 13, 1925.

12   Correspondence, P. Sefton to T. W. Case, August 23, 1925.

13   CRL Notebook 13, September 24, 1925, p. 7. Out of this request, Wall started John M. Wall Inc., a movie camera manufacturing company. His equipment was used by Pathé News, Movietone News, and other film industry interests, as well as various governments. Wall became the premier manufacturer of cameras for the sound film industry. His last invention was the three-faced Cinerama camera in 1958. "John M. Wall Dies; Movie Camera Maker," *Syracuse Herald-Journal*, July 24, 1963, p. 36; and other newspaper clippings from the collections of the Onondaga Historical Association, Syracuse, New York.

14   Sponable's comment about "quite bad" films was a sarcastic reference to De Forest Phonofilm. In de Forest's system, the projector had a sound head above the projection head. When Case and de Forest ended their collaboration, Case and Sponable moved the sound head in their projector to below the projection head. Sponable admitted later that moving the sound head may have been unnecessary. Sponable, transcript of lecture, given at Columbia University, December 14, 1937. Sponable Collection.

15   Correspondence, T. W. Case to J. F. Dulles, September 11, 1925.

16   Correspondence, T. W. Case to Lee de Forest, September 25, 1925.

17   CRL Notebook 13, September 29, 1925, p. 14.

18   Correspondence, Benjamin Castle to T. W. Case, October 2, 1925.

19   Correspondence, D. B. Eldred to J. F. Dulles, October 3, 1925.

20   Telegram, J. F. Dulles to T. W. Case, October 15, 1925.

21   CRL Notebook 13, October 16, 1925, pp. 33-35. Correspondence, D. B. Eldred to George Compton, November 27, 1925. The parade of Phonofilms board members, reviews of meetings, and correspondence regarding the Case-de Forest negotiations are covered extensively in Case's notes, and in correspondence files with de Forest, Dulles, and Phonofilms board members Bolster, Castle, and Compton.

22   Correspondence, Lee de Forest to T. W. Case, November 21, 1925.

23   Notes on de Forest negotiations, November-December 1925.

24   Meeting notes, De Forest Phonofilms, November 30, 1925. Eldred wrote across the top, "This given to me by Mr. Harold Bolster in presence of Dr. De Forest on Dec. 4, 1925 as a true copy of the minutes of the Board of Directors meeting of the De Forest Phonofilm Corp. held during week of Nov. 30, 1925."

25   Correspondence, J. F. Dulles to T. W. Case, December 11, 1925.

26   Correspondence, D. B. Eldred to George Compton, December 9, 1925.

Chapter 7

1   Sponable, "Historical Development of Sound Film," *SMPE Journal* 48: 4-5, April and May 1947, p. 297.

2   CRL Notebook 13, December 17, 1925, p. 40.

3   De Forest Patent No. 1482119 and Ries Patent No. 1473976. Ries had visited the Case Research Lab in 1923, and offered to sell Case his patents for $1000. But Case declined.

4   CRL Notebook 13, January 7, 1926, p. 44. During a trip to Western Electric's New York studio, Case and Sponable heard their system of sound-on-film and commented that music reproduced very well but talking was not good. CRL Notebook 13, January 29, 1926, pp. 53-54. Despite believing that Case's system was not useful for Western Electric (Case's technology was already further ahead), Craft asked to know more about it.

5   CRL Notebook 13, April 7, 1926, p. 80.

6   Correspondence, D. B. Eldred to T. W. Case, April 26, 1926. Case did not record his hesitations about working with Pathé, but Hayden, Stone and Co. had agreed to back a deal up to half a million dollars.

7   Sponable, "Historical Development of Sound Films," *SMPE Journal* 48: 4-5, April and May 1947, pp. 301-302.

Footnotes

8   MacGowan, Kenneth, *Behind the Screen* (New York: Dell Publishing, 1965), p. 283.

9   Correspondence, Joe Daly to D. B. Eldred, May 17, 1926.

10 Correspondence, Walter A. Darby, Darby & Darby, to The Wm. Fox Theatres, May 14, 1926. Copy of registered letter given to Case by Courtland Smith.

11 Correspondence, C. Smith, Fox Theatres Corporation, to T. W. Case, May 17, 1926; Memo to J. Leo and C. Smith, from D. B. Eldred, "DeForest against Fox," May 20, 1926.

12 Sponable, "Historical Development of Sound Films," *SMPE Journal* 48:4-5, April and May 1947, p. 302.

13 Sponable, transcript of lecture given at Columbia University, December 14, 1937, p. 2. Sponable Collection.

14 Case turned over five U.S. patents, eleven Canadian patents, thirteen British patents, thirteen French patents, fourteen Belgian patents, six Spanish patents, two Indian patents, two New Zealand patents, three Swiss patents, thirty-four U.S. pending applications, and fourteen pending foreign applications.

15 "Phonofilms Sues Fox Movietone Patents," *New York Morning Telegraph*, August 1926. Article pasted into Case scrapbook.

16 Fox-Case memorandum, October 26, 1926. Sponable Collection.

17 "Meeting on Talking Motion Pictures," notes on meeting with representatives of Fox-Case, General Electric, Westinghouse, and RCA, October 29, 1926.

18 Correspondence, Allan Porter, Museum of Modern Art, to E. I. Sponable, December 21, 1937, and Sponable, transcript of lecture given at Columbia University, December 14, 1937, p. 19. Sponable Collection.

19 "Fox Film Corporation Patent Situation in Sound Field," 1933, opening section, pp. 6-7. A comprehensive patent memorandum prepared in 1933, following several reorganizations of Fox Films, and in preparation of General Talking Pictures suit regarding the de Forest patents. Sponable Collection.

20 Correspondence, D. B. Eldred to T. W. Case, December 10, 1926.

21 Sponable felt that Fox did not pursue sound film aggressively enough until after the Vitaphone premier. Sponable, transcript of lecture given at Columbia University, Dec. 14, 1937, p. 20. Sponable Collection.

22 Eileen Creelman, "Picture Plays & Players," *New York Evening Sun*, February 25, 1927. Pasted into Case's scrapbook along with Eldred's note and numerous other clippings covering the screening.

23 The Movietone short of Lindbergh was the first sound sensation, while Warner brothers' *The Jazz Singer* was the first feature film sensation. Will Hays, *See and Hear* (New York: Motion Picture Producers and Distributors of American, 1929), p. 53. Author Benjamin Hampton later called the Lindbergh short "a momentous event in motion picture history." Benjamin Hampton, *History of the American Film Industry* (New York: Dover Publications, 1970) p. 383.

24 Fox Film Corporation Patent Situation in Sound Field," Section V, pp. 11-12. Sponable Collection.

25 "Movietone versus Phonofilm," *The Screen Press*, Volume 1 No. 24, June 25, 1927, p. 4.

Chapter 8

1 CRL Notebook 15, entries for August 29, 1929, p. 138; Nov. 13, 1929, p. 144; and July 2, 1930, p. 162.

2 Correspondence, Courtland Smith to William Fox, November 13, 1928.

3 Undated notes regarding clarification points of Case Research Lab role and Case's position within the organization, circa 1928. Sponable Collection.

4 "Brief Report for Mr. Fox of work done at the Case Research Lab, Inc. during year 1928-1929." Copy of report in Case correspondence, 1929.

5 Sponable helped perfect the Western Electric sound-on-film system. After the deals were signed, Fox-Case and Western Electric carried out joint investigative work in the Fox-Case laboratories. "Fox Film Corporation Patent Situation in Sound Field," 1933, section I, pp. 4, 9-10. Sponable Collection. Also, due to Fox's agreements with ERPI, all Fox Films include the line "produced using Western Electric Equipment" in their credits, even though until 1930 they used the Movietone system for the recording process.

6 "Fox Film Corporation Patent Situation in Sound Field," 1933, section V, p. 2. Sponable Collection.

7 David A. Cook, *A History of Narrative Film* (New York: W. W. Norton and Co., 1981), p. 245.

8 It was later claimed that the meeting minutes in which the deal was ratified were faked. The five directors who voted in favor of it had personal ties to William Fox or Fox Films. "Fox Film Corporation Patent Situation in Sound Field," 1933, section I, p. 13. Sponable Collection.

9 The deal in 1929 involved taking the stock in Fox-Case Corporation and turning it over to two new corporations, one of Eldred and Sponable (as Fox representatives) and the other of the Case Research Lab Incorporated (T. W. and Gertrude Case, Sefton, Taber, Eldred, and Sponable). The final breakdown of funds by Case and the associates in the film development, received after stock transferals, etc, was as follows: Theodore W. Case (for loans to the Case Research Lab), $118,980; Theodore W.

Footnotes

Case (for his original personal investment), $803,280; Getrude E. Case, $107,100; Pennington Sefton, $107,100; John Taber, $53,580; Dwight B. Eldred, $124,980; and Earl I. Sponable, $184,980.

10 Fox Hearst Corporation later became Movietonenews, Inc. "Fox Film Corporation Patent Situation in Sound Field," February 1933, section I, p. 18; Exh. 15, p. 1. Sponable Collection.

11 At the same time Fox acquired Loew's, he bought a 45 percent share in British-Gaumont, the largest film organization in England. In 1927, Fox had purchased rights to the Tri-Ergon patents, and he formed American Tri-Ergon to commercialize that system as well. "Fox Film Patent Situation in Sound Field," 1933, opening section, p. 15, and "addenda," pp. 1-10. In October 1929, the stock market crashed. A month later, at the urging of Louis B. Mayer, (the MGM production head who was closely associated with the Hoover administration) the Justice Department ordered Fox to divest himself of the Loew's stock. AT & T (as parent company of Western Electric and ERPI) and Wall Street interests were also involved in reigning in Fox's power. David Cook, *A History of Narrative Film*, p. 244-245; Stephen M. Silverman, *The Fox That Got Away* (Secaucus, New Jersey: Lyle Stuart Inc., 1988), pp. 54-56; and Tino Balio, ed. *The American Film Industry*, pp. 250-251. Fox presented his own version of events in a book written by Upton Sinclair, *Upton Sinclair Presents William Fox* (New York: Sinclair, 1933). A later Tri-Ergon patent, "Devices for Phonographs with Linear Phonogram Carriers," that was assigned to William Fox by Tri-Ergon's inventors in 1929 is in the Sponable Collection at the Cayuga Museum.

12 "Fox Film Patent Situation in Sound Field," 1933, section II, p. 10. Sponable Collection.

13 Correspondence, E. I. Sponable to Harley Clarke, June 14, 1930. Sponable Collection.

14 Report of Case-Sponable-Cloud Developments, Inter-Office Correspondence, F. R. Moulton to Harley Clarke, August 10, 1930, p. 4. Sponable Collection.

15 Ibid., p. 4.

16 Kellogg, Peter Paul, "A Study of Bird Song Recordings," Ph.D. dissertation. Presented to the faculty of the Graduate School of Cornell University. February 1938. Pp. 64-65. Eventually the crew went to Cornell, and completed the first synchronized film recordings of wild birds in their natural habitat. Kellogg thanked Sponable and Sefton for assistance with the project in his acknowledgements.

17 Recollections of Jane Case, written on photographs given to the Cayuga Museum. The boathouse and its contents, including the steamer *Dorothy*, were destroyed by fire in the late 1930s.

18 CRL Notebook 16, Nov. 19, 1931, p. 12.

19 Correspondence, E. I. Sponable, Fox Film Corporation, to T. W. Case, April 23, 1932. Sponable Collection.

20 Sponable, "Historical Development of Sound Films," *SMPE Journal* 48: 4-5, April and May 1947, p. 408.

Glossary of Technical and Scientific Terms

Aeo light

a vacuum tube containing a mixture of gases that was extremely sensitive to sound vibrations; also described as a gas glow tube and a modulated glow lamp. Aeo stands for alkaline earth oxides, a reference to the oxides that coated the light's platinum cathode. Initially called the helio-light, the Aeo light served as the sensitive recording source in Case's sound film system.

Air-thermo microphone

a microphone created by the Case Research Lab that used an air jet and manometric flame (see definition on the following page). The air-thermo microphone was an experimental part of the sound film recording apparatus in 1923.

Arc

a band of sparks or incandescent light formed when electric discharge is conducted from one conducting surface to another. Arc searchlights, part of the Case Research Lab's infrared system, used arc rods made of carbon as the lighting mechanism.

Audion

a small incandescent electric lamp or tube that detected wireless waves, invented in 1906 by Lee de Forest, who called it "a new receiver for wireless telegraphy." An Audion Amplifier used audion bulbs in the detection of electrical signals.

Barium

a silver-white slightly malleable chemical element. Case used an oxide of barium in the large vacuum tubes that were part of the daylight recording system.

Cover glass

part of the sound recording apparatus in the Case Research Lab sound camera. A very thin piece of glass served as a protective cover over the slit on the recording mechanism, to help prevent dirt from marring recordings.

Galvanometer
a scientific instrument used to detect and measure a small electric current. Three different types of galvanometers exist in the Case Research Lab objects collection.

Helio-light
Case's original name for the Aeo light

Infrared
invisible rays beyond the red end of the spectrum, longer than the spectrum colors but shorter than radio waves. The rays were invisible to the human eye but could be picked up by substances sensitive to the red and infrared parts of the spectrum.

Kinetophone
a sound on disc system invented in 1913 by Thomas Edison, that played briefly in four New York theaters. It used an oversized wax disk and a system of belts and pulleys between the projection booth and the stage to synchronize sound and image. Edison successfully demonstrated the system, but when used commercially, it was almost impossible to keep the sound in sync with the image. By 1914, Kinetophone proved a failure and Edison never again tried his hand at talking pictures.

Kuntz cell
a photoelectric cell invented by Jacob Kuntz in 1913, used by Lee de Forest in his early sound film experiments.

Latent image
an image perhaps capable of existence that is unseen; the idea that an impression of the last thing seen remains momentarily on the retina of the eye.

Leeds & Northrup Co.
a scientific equipment company based in Philadelphia that manufactured such products as galvanometers and dial resistance boxes. The Case Research Lab purchased equipment from them, and cooperated with them in marketing the daylight recording system.

Luminescence
emission of light by processes that derive energy from nonthermal sources; certain solid substances emit light when excited

Manometric flame
a gas jet arranged so that sound vibrations produce changes in the gas supplied to the jet; a modulated oxy-acetylene flame used by Case in early sound transmission experiments, and later used in sound film work.

Oxidizing

to unite with oxygen, as in burning or rusting; to remove electrons from a substance. Lab workers often oxidized substances used as coating elements on filaments in the light cells.

Parabolic Lens

a concave lens having the shape of a parabola (a plane curve formed by a conial section taken parallel to an element of the intersected cone). The Case Research Lab used a parabolic lens as part of early experimental prototypes for the infrared signaling system.

Paraffining

to coat with wax (to make wood surfaces more waterproof)

Pathé Studios

Pathé Fréres, a French company, one of the early film pioneers. They proved a prolific producer of films during the reign of silent films, and began producing and running weekly newsreels in 1910.

Persistence of vision

the continuance of an effect after the effect is removed. When the eye sees an image, the brain retains that image for a moment longer. This "after image" fuses with the next one in a person's mind. Persistence of vision is how the individual frames in a filmstrip merge into a moving image.

Phosphorescence

persistent emission of light following exposure to and removal of incident radiation, causing a substance to "glow in the dark."

Photion tube

De Forest's name for a gas glow discharge tube he worked on in the late 1910s. He also used this term to refer to the light cell Case invented which became the Aeo light.

Photoelectricity

of or having to do with electric effects produced by light or other radiation, as in emission of electrons by substances when subjected to light or radiation of a suitable wavelength; a substance or device has the ability to change light into an electric action.

Photoelectric cells

a cell whose electrical state is changed by the effect of light.

Photometer

an instrument used for measuring a property of light, especially luminous intensity.

Potentiometer

an instrument for recording or measuring an unknown voltage or potential difference by comparison to a standard voltage. The Case Research Lab used a potentiometer in the daylight recording system.

Ries Patents

Elias E. Ries filed an application in 1913 for a very broad patent covering a sound-on-film system that was granted in 1923. Ries' patent described almost every aspect of systems that were later brought to reality by other inventors. There was little evidence that all parts of Ries' inventions worked, but patent laws at the time were very broad. The Ries patents, which Lee de Forest purchased in 1925, proved problematic during the patent wars in sound film's early commercial history.

Selenium

discovered in 1817, a substance that exhibits photoconductivity; shows photoelectric effect only in gray crystalline form. It was often used in photoelectric cells until inventors like Case found that thallium compounds could be better, more stable conductors.

Strontium

a pale yellow metallic compound discovered in 1808 that burns with a red flame. The Case Research Lab used strontium as a coating on filaments in vacuum tubes for the daylight recording system.

Thallium

a rare, poisonous bluish-gray soft metallic element used in making photoelectric cells and rat poison. Case used thallium salts and thallium sulfide in perfecting the Thalofide Cell.

Thalofide Cell

a photoelectric cell invented by Theodore Case. Sensitive to red and infrared, and more sensitive and dynamic in response than selenium cells.

Tri-Ergon

the name for a sound-on-film process that used a modulated glow discharge for recording and a photocell for reproducing. Tri-Ergon, meaning literally "the work of three" was invented by three Swiss-Germans, Josef Engl, Joseph Massolle, and Hans Vogt, who began working on it in 1918. Tri-Ergon eventually became the most powerful film company in Germany and dominated the market in the early sound era.

Selected Bibliography

This list is not meant as a definitive bibliography of sound film. The following sources are among those used in the research on this publication, and will be of interest to those who want to learn more about the early days of sound and the motion picture industry.

Allvine, Glendon. *The Greatest Fox of Them All.* New York: Lyle Stuart, 1969.

Balio, Tino, ed. *The American Film Industry.* Madison, Wisconsin: University of Wisconsin Press, 1976; revised 1985.

Carneal, Georgette. *A Conqueror of Space: The Life of Lee de Forest.* New York: Horace Liveright, 1930.

Cook, David A. *A History of Narrative Film.* New York: W. W. Norton and Co., 1981.

Everson, William K. *American Silent Film.* New York: Oxford University Press, 1978.

Eyman, Scott. *The Speed of Sound: Hollywood and the Talkie Revolution, 1926-1930.* New York: Simon & Schuster, 1997.

Geduld, Harry M. *The Birth of The Talkies.* Bloomington, Indiana: Indiana University Press, 1975.

Hampton, Benjamin B. *History of the American Film Industry.* New York: Dover Publications, 1970.

Hays, Will H. *See and Hear.* New York: Motion Picture Producers and Distributors of America, Inc., 1929.

Kellogg, Edward W. "History of Sound Motion Pictures." *Journal of Society of Motion Picture and Television Engineers.* Volume 64. Reprint from June, July, and August 1955.

Knight, Arthur. *The Liveliest Art.* New York: New American Library, 1957.

Kraft, James P. *Stage to Studio: Musicians and the Sound Revolution, 1890-1950.* Baltimore: The Johns Hopkins University Press, 1996.

Lewis, Howard T. *The Motion Picture Industry.* New York: D. Van Nostrand Company, 1933.

Lewis, Tom. *Empire of the Air: The Men Who Made Radio.* New York: HarperCollins, 1991.

McGowan, Kenneth. *Behind the Screen.* New York: Delacourte Press, 1965.

Ries, Estelle H. *Elias E. Ries, Inventor.* New York: Philosophical Library, 1951.

Silverman, Stephen M. *The Fox That Got Away.* Secaucus, New Jersey: Lyle Stuart, Inc., 1988.

Sinclair, Upton. *Upton Sinclair Presents William Fox.* New York: Sinclair, 1933.

Sponable, Earl. "Historical Development of Sound Films." *Journal of the Society of Motion Picture Engineers,* Volume 48. Numbers 4-5, April and May, 1947.

Walker, Alexander. *The Shattered Silents.* New York: William Morrow and Co., 1979.

Zworkin, V. K., and Ramberg, E. G. *Photo-Electricity.* New York: John Wiley and Sons, 1949.

Zworkin, V. K., and Wilson, E. D. *Photocells and Their Applications.* New York: John Wiley and Sons, 1930.

Index

Index

Index

THALOFIDE CELL

HIGH VACUUM, HELIUM OR HYDROGEN FILLED

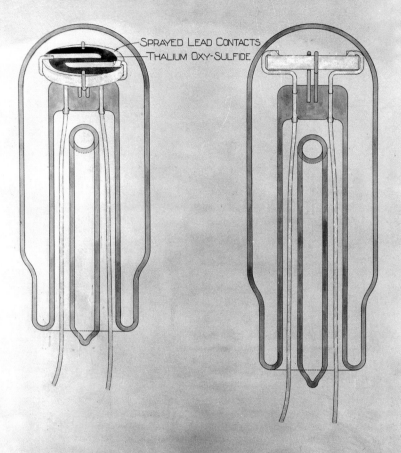

SPRAYED LEAD CONTACTS
THALIUM OXY-SULFIDE

CASE RESEARCH LABORATORY INC.
AUBURN, N.Y.

Acknowledgements

Preliminary work for this publication began in 1996 when the Cayuga Museum initiated a three-part documentation project for the collections of the Case Research Lab. From 1996 through 1998, staff undertook the time-consuming process of accessioning, researching, and cataloguing the valuable technological history. *Breaking the Silence on Film*, the result of this process, is based on the Case Research Lab objects and archival collections at the Cayuga Museum.

Fortunately for scholars, Case maintained good records of lab activities. Primary source materials used in this project include twenty-three laboratory notebooks and volumes of technical drawings (dating from 1916-1934), extensive business and personal correspondence, manuscripts and reports prepared for publication and contract negotiations, patents, receipts, equipment catalogues, and scrapbooks of newspaper clippings that Case diligently compiled in the 1920s. Additional research sources include archival materials from Earl Sponable, which were graciously donated to the Cayuga Museum by his daughter, Catherine "Mimo" Sponable, in the 1990s. These materials are housed at the Cayuga Museum.

I could not have undertaken this project without help from many individuals, and could not have completed it without the support of many others. My sincere thanks to Marie Eckhardt, who patiently inventoried, cleaned, accessioned, and numbered hundreds of objects included in the Case Research Lab collection. Marie spent many additional hours of detective work in the archival collections of the Cayuga Museum and Cornell University, tracking down the genealogy of the Case family, the beginnings of the Case Research Lab, Earl Sponable's background, and possible Cornell University connections to the lab's founding. Chapters 1 and 2 are the result of her research and writing. I also extend thanks to Paul Doering, who provided valuable expertise in early sound film technology, and displayed endless patience in discussing and identifying equipment and mysterious devices with Marie and me in marathon research sessions throughout 1997.

My sincere thanks also to Executive Director Jim Richerson, who has been a strong supporter of this project since his arrival at the Cayuga Museum in May 1997. Jim's contribution to this publication, *Every Building Tells a Story*, tracks the chronology of the Case Research Lab buildings, and documents the process that led to the site's preservation and interpretation through 1998.

This project could not have been undertaken without the support of the New York State Council on the Arts, which from 1996 through 1998 provided substantial financial backing. My thanks specifically to NYSCA representatives Don Palmer and Kristin Herron, who ably represented this project to the Council and enthusiastically supported it through three development phases.

I owe a debt of gratitude to Cayuga Museum staff members Jessica Kline, Lynn Palmieri, and Lydia Rosell, who gave me the opportunity to dedicate a large portion of my time in 1998-1999 to writing this publication. I also express my thanks to the Cayuga Museum Board of Trustees, who have supported this project from the beginning. Thanks to Laura Coburn of Coburn Design for her expertise and enthusiasm in work on the design and layout of this book, which wonderfully complements the visual nature of the material.

I am indebted to several individuals for reading through various phases of the manuscript, and for providing valuable suggestions, comments and corrections. These included Al Balk, David Connelly, Paul Doering, Kristin Herron, Peter Jones, George Kerstetter, Leslie Przybylek and Ellen Baker Wikstrom.

Contents

This book is respectfully dedicated
to the memory of
Theodore W. Case and his family,
a tribute long overdue.